Voyageur Press titles are also available at discounts in bulk quantity for industrial or sales-promotional use. For details write to Special Sales Manager at Quarto Publishing Group USA Inc., 400 First Avenue North, Suite 400, Minneapolis, MN 55401 USA.

To find out more about our books, visit us online at www.voyageurpress.com.

Library of Congress Cataloging-in-Publication Data

King, Bryan, 1974-
   12 Bones Smokehouse : a mountain BBQ cookbook / Bryan King, Angela King, Shane Heavner, Mackensy Lunsford.
      pages cm
   Includes index.
   ISBN 978-0-7603-4726-3 (paperback)
   1. Barbecuing. 2. Side dishes (Cooking) 3. 12 Bones Smokehouse. I. King, Angela, 1977- II. Heavner, Shane. III. Lunsford, Mackensy. IV. Title. V. Title: Twelve Bones Smokehouse.
   TX840.B3K4525 2015
   641.5'784--dc23
                          2014044799

Acquisitions Editor: Thom O'Hearn
Art Director: James Kegley
Page Design: Kim Winscher
Photography: Taylor Mathis
Photograph page 33: Pattiy Torno

Printed in China

10 9 8 7 6 5 4 3 2

12 BONES

smokehouse

A MOUNTAIN BBQ COOKBOOK

King, Heavner, and Lunsford

Voyageur
Press

CONTENTS

Foreword

12 Bones Smokehouse began its life in the belly of a squat and unassuming cinder block shack. It was square in the middle of a floodplain in Asheville, North Carolina. In fact, the building was still filled with river scum after it had lost its last restaurant—a greasy spoon frequented by warehouse workers and dump truck drivers—to chest-high floodwaters. The previous owner simply gave up.

The founders, Tom Montgomery and Sabra Kelley, cleaned things up, hung a few signs, and got the smoker running. They hoped to lure a little more than a hundred diners into the restaurant daily with the sweet smell of smoked meat and a marquis outside advertising "Tender Butts and Sweet Racks."

Partly due to that sign, Sabra says the first calls to the restaurant were from people asking if they were opening a strip club. But by the time Tom and Sabra passed the restaurant on to current owners Bryan and Angela King, the transformation of 12 Bones was nearly unfathomable.

In those intervening years, Barack and Michelle Obama had eaten 12 Bones' sweet racks three times. But they weren't the only fans. The little 'cue shack that could began pushing close to a thousand customers some days. The entire neighborhood around the restaurant continued to change as well. Boutique restaurants and breweries became a stone's throw away instead of a car's drive. But the restaurant has stayed more or less the same place it always was: a quirky little joint where people eat off metal plates and write on the walls.

When it comes to style, 12 Bones makes no apologies and declares no major allegiances. Want to argue about what city makes the best barbecue? That's all fine and good, but 12 Bones makes room under its roof for all types. Just like the restaurant, in this book you'll find odes to Memphis-style 'cue sitting beside a sauce that would be right at home in eastern Carolina—then turn the page and there's a recipe or two that would make folks from Kansas City smile. Of course there's also that rib sauce made with blueberries and chipotles, which might just be as close as you can get to Asheville-style barbecue.

So let the purists be the purists, fire up the grill, and enjoy some Southern 'cue, 12 Bones style.

—Mackensy Lunsford

Introduction

Over the years we have been asked some pretty funny questions at the restaurant: Are these old family recipes? Did President Obama have to pay for his meal? Can you ship ribs to California? What is that spice in the cornbread? Was this building underwater during the flood?

You'll find most of the answers, at least regarding the recipes, in this book.

Some of the recipes honor old family traditions, some are stolen from former places of employment and some are pure "I-need-a-special-for-today" last-minute genius. On the pages that follow, you'll see a recipe for vinegar slaw that came from Sabra's great-grandmother, Lilly Brightman, around 1890 in Kentucky. Our corn pudding, on the other hand, was the brainchild of Ron Brannon. He started 12 Bones with us, and many of the original recipes were ones that he and Tom perfected in the weeks before we opened by asking, usually at 3 a.m., "What else can we throw into this smoker?" (Sadly, Ron passed away before we got famous. He would have loved the notoriety.)

12 Bones has always been about the food and not much else. Luckily, when you open a restaurant focused on flavor alone, it is easy to inspire your staff as a team. And when you're on the 12 Bones team, we don't care if you have neck tattoos or wear a "Mullet Styles of the World" T-shirt, just as long as you can expertly prepare our delicious ribs the exact same way for 700 customers on a Tuesday. Piercings? We generally don't trust people who work in the restaurant industry who don't have them.

That may sound crazy, but it's worked pretty well for us over the years. Everyone concentrates on the food and, for the most part, customers and staff alike enjoy the experience.

So much so, that sometimes people stick around for quite a while. After eating here a few times, and much personal introspection, Bryan and Angela moved from the tech world of Silicon Valley to the slower pace of Asheville in late 2011. Without much restaurant experience, they got a crash course in everything 12 Bones, learning every position from the dish pit to the smoker before taking over as owners. What can we say? 12 Bones seems to inspire a certain sort of devotion.

good, fast pig

So it is with Chef Shane Heavner, who was raised about an hour away from here. He learned to cook from his great aunts and further honed his education at the Asheville-Buncombe Technical Community College Culinary Program at age 30. He joined the 12 Bones family in 2008 and became an integral part of everything we do around here. Many recipes in this book, in fact, belong to Shane.

We hope you enjoy this cookbook. It will at least answer the question of the spice in the cornbread. It also may just save you from the disastrous experience of shipping ribs. Oh, and don't take our treatise on 'cue as gospel; make sure to experiment a little with the recipes yourself. That's how we got here, after all.

Enjoy y'all,

Bryan and Angela King (owners),
Tom Montgomery and Sabra Kelley (founders),
Shane Heavner (chef), and the rest of the 12 Bones family

I the essentials

With some of the recipes in this book—most of the meat-based recipes, in fact—nailing the cooking method is as important as buying the proper ingredients. While you don't need major grill know-how, if you want to make some of the ribs, briskets, and other barbecue basics, you'll want to brush up on the tips and techniques in this chapter. You'll also learn a little bit about what kind of tools you'll need to execute the recipes ahead.

★ TOOLS OF THE TRADE

Grill brush: You need to cook your meat on a clean surface. End of story.

Tongs: Every cook worth his or her salt needs a good pair of tongs. No wimpy ice tongs, either. Invest in one—or several—spring-loaded, stainless steel tongs. If you're going to be turning lots of pieces of meat on a screaming-hot grill, your arms will thank you later for purchasing an extra-long set.

Metal spatula: Tongs don't play well with everything. There are times you'll need a spatula to flip smaller pieces of meat on the grill.

Microplane: A microplane, essentially a surgical-grade steel grater, will end up being your best friend. It's essential for zesting citrus fruits and grating hard cheeses and chocolate.

Kitchen towels and good grill gloves: Forget about those fancy kitchen towels. You need a good, solid stack of workhorse towels that can carry a hot pot, grease a grill grate, and mop up any mess you make. Grill gloves provide extra protection for your hands.

Nonstick silicone mat: While this isn't exactly essential, it's a great tool to have on hand, particularly if you're going to delve into the process of baking (see Chocolate Chip Cookies on page 196). These mats are reusable, washable, withstand incredibly high temperatures (check manufacturer's details), and are nonstick, even without the addition of extra fats.

Basting brushes and mops: Want to keep your meat from drying out? Baste, baste, and baste again. A proper mop for barbecuing and some sturdy basting brushes are both useful in their own way.

Spice grinder: Sure it's not a grill tool, but a spice grinder is helpful to have on hand to make many of the spice rubs we've included in this book. Rub recipes start on page 26.

Metal fire shovel: If you're going to be moving coals around, you'll need a fire-safe implement to get the job done. We've been known to use extra-long tongs, too.

Disposable foil pans: You can use these to create a makeshift smoker box. You can also use them as disposable containers in which to rub your meats.

Thermometers: For many of these recipes, you'll need a meat thermometer if you can't judge the doneness of meat by touch alone. For some recipes, a candy thermometer would be helpful, particularly when trying to gauge the temperature of frying oil.

Meat thermometers get put through the ringer, so invest in a sturdy one. Also, we suggest getting a nice oven thermometer so you can get a more accurate read on the heat of your grill, right where you're cooking the meat. Many backyard grills have a built-in thermometer, but they're often situated a little too far above the cooking surface to get an accurate feel for what's going on down on the grill grates.

Quart containers, jars with lids, and other sealable storage containers: Some of these recipes, particularly the sauces, aren't meant to be used in one fell swoop. Same goes with the pickles. Make sure that you have plenty of clean storage containers to deal with the leftovers. Plastic quart containers—the kind in which you might get takeout noodle soup—are perfect. They handle hot temperatures fine, to a degree. They're washable and reusable. And they stack up nicely in the refrigerator or freezer. That's why chefs order them by the sleeve. Spend enough time around us, and you'll realize that we use them for just about everything—even drinking cups, in a pinch.

★ SMOKING YOUR MEAT

Firewood is one of the oldest cooking tools in the world, and cooking over wood is a satisfying way of rendering meat into something extraordinary. In a post-microwave world, you know something's a good thing when it's complicated yet still a go-to technique.

Wood smoke, imparted to meat cooked low and slow, is at the heart of the barbecue mystique. The true flavor of the pit is best obtained with a smoker. Though they have a reputation for being expensive, you can obtain a basic smoker from your local hardware store with a minimal investment. Of course, the price climbs as you add bulk and other bells and whistles.

The premise of any smoker is basically the same: It cooks food in a smoke-filled, enclosed environment conducive to low and slow cooking. While that may sound straightforward, it's trickier than it seems. With a basic home oven, cranking the temperature up or down is as easy as a flick of the wrist and a twist of a dial. With wood, it's more complicated. It takes time, knowledge of your smoker, and a whole lot of trial and error. Of course, some smokers come with temperature control, which makes things a bit easier.

Here at 12 Bones, we're used to the whims and wants of our sometimes persnickety smokers, and we know what tricks and techniques will coax them into merrily huffing and puffing along. We have a lot of mouths to feed—fast—but the home cook has the benefit of time. (At least we hope you don't have lines of people gathered outside your door first thing in the morning waiting to be fed like we do!)

If you're using a new smoker, take some time getting to know it before you invite the neighborhood over. Try a few dry runs with a heat-safe thermometer until you know what you can expect from different areas of your smoker (particularly important if using an offset smoker). Figure out what kind of fuel you need. Read the manufacturer's instructions. It won't kill you.

If you don't have a smoker, that's perfectly fine; there are other ways to get that sweet, sweet taste of smoke on your ribs, butts, and briskets.

★ COOKING OVER GAS

For all of the naysayers out there, we still think gas grills have plenty going for them. Heck, at 12 Bones we use gas grills, in addition to our smokers, every day. For one, it's quite easy to control the temperature of a gas grill, and most of our recipes call for fairly precise temperatures (though straying ever so slightly out of the ranges in the recipes will, in most cases, be perfectly fine).

For many of the slow-cooking techniques you'll find in this book, indirect heat is the key. If you have a gas grill, turn off half of the burners and set your racks (or brisket, or what-have-you) over the cooler side of the grill to cook them indirectly.

How you add smoke to a gas grill is where things get a bit more complicated, but it's definitely doable. Some gas grills come with smoker boxes, but if not, purchasing one is a great investment. Fill your box with wood chips that have been presoaked for about 30 minutes, and place the box directly under the grill grates, on the lit burner, and close the lid of the grill tight to seal in the smoke. If you have a built-in smoker box, make sure to light the burner underneath it. You can also create your own smoker box by filling an aluminum pan with soaked chips and covering the pan with foil. Poke a few holes in the foil, and you're ready to go.

While using the indirect heat method to cook your meat, close the lid of the grill to allow the smoke and heat to circulate, creating something of a smoky, convection-oven environment. Don't open the lid any more than necessary to baste and check on the status of your wood. In cold weather, opening the lid increases cooking time.

When you're cooking with wood chips, it's likely you'll have to replenish them throughout the cooking process, particularly for recipes with longer cooking times. Just keep a pot of presoaked chips near the grill for that very purpose. If your chips catch on fire, toss a tiny bit of water on the flame to extinguish it and close that lid back up tight. The chips should go back to smoking quickly.

Wood chunks are larger than chips and better suited to longer periods of cooking, as their larger size means they don't burn up as quickly. Place your wood chunks in larger smoker boxes or even directly on the grates of a gas grill.

★ COOKING OVER CHARCOAL

When it comes to grilling over charcoal, you have choices. A tour of any hardware store makes that abundantly clear. You'll find "cowboy charcoal," made with mesquite wood, next to eco-friendly briquettes made with coconut shells bound with tapioca. You'll also see self-lighting and natural, hardwood lump charcoal. How do you pick one?

It's mostly a personal choice. We use wood to smoke our meats, but we've also been known to throw a party or three in the parking lot of 12 Bones. And for those occasions, we like to use traditional charcoal briquettes to which we add pieces of wood once the coals are good and

how to get
perfect grill marks
EVERYTIME
USING DIRECT HEAT

Grill marks are purely a matter of aesthetics, but sometimes you just want that picture-perfect steak. Here's how the pros do it. This only applies to higher-heat methods of cooking.

Step 1: Heat.

Make sure your grill is screaming hot so you get a good sear on your meat. However, make sure to keep a "cool zone" where you can move your pieces of meat to finish cooking after you mark those babies up just right.

Step 2: Lubricate.

Make sure either your food, your grates—or both—are oiled up, without going overboard, of course.

Step 3: Placement.

Set your food on the grill grates at about a 45-degree angle or, say, pointing to 10 o'clock. Sear. Rotate a quarter turn, or to about 7 o'clock, and sear again. Flip, again angling the meat 45 degrees. Point this time to 2 o'clock. Sear. Then rotate 90 degrees. Move to the cool side to cook or, if you're cooking something quickly, like a rare steak, remove from heat and rest.

hot. We like the consistent size of briquettes, which means consistent burn times and even temperatures. Charcoal briquettes are also readily available and fairly inexpensive.

You have a few choices to make when it comes to lighting your charcoal. Self-lighting charcoal is presoaked in lighter fluid. That's fine, but you can control the amount of fluid you use if you purchase charcoal that's not presoaked—or you can skip the lighter fluid altogether.

If you're using lighter fluid, pile your briquettes in a big heap, apply the lighter fluid, making sure to coat all of the coals, and let it soak into the briquettes for about 5 minutes. That way, when you light your fire, the fuel won't be as likely to burn right off. And you definitely don't want to throw extra fuel on a fire that's already lit.

After lighting the pile, give the coals a little stir after the flames die down. If you don't move your coals around, allowing oxygen to permeate the pile, some of the coals might not catch and burn at the same rate as the rest. Once the briquettes are glowing and covered with a light coating of ash, they're ready to go. That takes about 30 minutes.

Even better, for a small investment you can purchase a charcoal chimney from your local hardware store. It's a great method for starting a fire without adding any lighter fluid. To get a fire started, first roll up four sheets of newspaper, twist the roll into a doughnut shape, and pack it under the grate of the chimney—not too tight, so air can still circulate. Then fill the top of the chimney with charcoal. Remove the grate from your charcoal grill, and set the filled chimney inside the grill. Next, light the paper and let the fire light the briquettes. Once the charcoal is glowing and covered with a fine coating of ash, turn your burning coals carefully into your grill, protecting your hands with heavy-duty oven mitts. Replace the grate and give the grill some time to warm up, just like preheating an oven. Be careful where you put that chimney; it will be hot.

The number one thing to remember about using charcoal briquettes is this: If you see a flame, it's not time to cook. Though the coals will look plenty hot, in reality, a flame means that the outside layer, including the lighter fluid (if you're using it) is still burning off—and you just don't want that in your food.

When we host events outside, we use seasoned hardwood logs to add smoke to the meat. We throw the wood on the coals as soon as they get that glowing amber color. Of course, we have to wait a while for the fire to break down the wood. The outside layer of the wood can be toxic, so we let the bark burn off first. When the wood is red and glowing, it's ready to cook with. If it still resembles a log, we let it go a bit longer. Sometimes, we'll even pre-burn the wood and then douse it with water to put the fire out and set it aside until grill time.

You can also add presoaked wood chips or chunks to the coals. Chunks are probably your best bet, as they don't burn up quite as quickly. If you use wood logs like we do, make sure those logs are seasoned properly (aged for at least a season to allow them to dry), and, more importantly, untreated. Never try to smoke food with wood you can't identify. Read on to learn more about what type of wood to use for cooking.

A word about indirect heat with charcoal grills: If you're planning to cook low and slow over charcoal, as you would for ribs, it's important to "bank" the coals. Simply put, that means pushing your pile of lit coals to one side, replacing the grate, and cooking your food over the side without the coals, with the lid of the grill closed tight so the smoke and heat can circulate around the meat. Use your grill vents to regulate the heat.

★ THE WORD ON WOOD

Here at 12 Bones, we use cherry wood to smoke our butts and briskets, and oak for pretty much everything else. Here's a basic guide to a handful of hardwoods that you might want to try out for flavor.

Cherry: Mild and fruity in flavor, cherry wood won't overpower your seasoning. Highly versatile, cherry will work for smoking just about anything and can be mixed with other woods. It matches well with some of the spices we use, particularly those in the 12 Bones Butt Rub (page 27).

Oak: With a medium flavor that's highly versatile, oak makes a perfect go-to wood to keep on hand. The flavor of oak mixes well with poultry, but it's strong enough to stand up to lamb. Try to find red oak, if you can. It also works just fine for dishes like the Smoked Shrimp on page 82.

Hickory: We don't use hickory at 12 Bones because of its intense flavor. It can quickly become overpowering, but if you want a strong, smoky flavor, and you aren't worried about letting the flavors from a rub come through, this is your wood. Also, you'll get more smoke flavor with less wood, so if you're just tossing some chips on your charcoal or gas grill, hickory is a good way to go. In our opinion, however, meat that spends too much time over hickory or mesquite can pick up a bitter flavor.

Apple: As anyone who has ever had applewood-smoked bacon can attest, this wood is excellent for pork, especially sausage (like the brats on page 44) and other cured meats.

Mesquite: This is another "aggressive" wood that, like hickory, provides a strong flavor. A little goes a long way, so mesquite works well as a complement to other woods or for just tossing a handful of chips on the grill for a quick hit of flavor.

Alder: This type of wood adds a more delicate, almost-sweet smoke flavor. It pairs perfectly with salmon and poultry.

★ BRINE: WHAT, WHY, AND HOW

At 12 Bones, we do a ton of brining, particularly with tougher cuts of meat. Injecting meat with marinades was a big fad for a while, and one we refused to take part in. Why? If you inject juices into meat, you're just spot treating, if you will. But soaking meat in brine—a solution of salt, sometimes other spices, and water—ensures that all your meat soaks up plenty of flavor. Of course, everyone has his or her own opinion on the matter.

As far as moisture goes, meat retains some of the liquid in which it's soaked. Of course, some of that liquid is lost during the cooking process. But brining meat causes a chemical reaction too. Salt breaks down the proteins in the cells of the meat, tenderizing the muscle fibers, which can contract while cooking and make meat tougher. In this process of breaking down proteins, the salt also allows the cells to soak up even more liquid. That's some delicious science.

> **SIMPLE BRINE RECIPE**
> • • • • • • • • • • •
> 2 quarts cold water
> ¾ cup kosher salt
> ½ cup brown sugar
> 2 pounds of ice

The recipes in this book that call for brining, such as the corned beef, pork loin, and pastrami, have the brine recipe included. But, for basic brine, we use the recipe at right and add seasonings as we see fit.

We combine the ingredients in a large pot and submerge the meat in the brine, then store the whole thing in our walk-in cooler. As you might imagine, that takes up a lot of space, and that's something you need to consider when brining at home. Brisket, for example, soaks for about 24 hours per every pound of meat, allowing the brine to work its magic throughout. Though that may sound like a long time to have meat bobbing around in salt water, brining actually helps preserve the meat too. Even our health inspector says we can brine our meat for up to two weeks, so soak away.

One word about brining: It makes your meat saltier, obviously. So watch the salt content of any rub or seasoning you'll add later.

the **10**
COMMANDMENTS
of GRILLING

Before we move on to the first recipes, we have some general advice based on all our years in the kitchen (and manning the smokers and grills). While a lot of techniques and seasoning may be subjective, this list is a collection of what's not up for debate at 12 Bones.

1 Thou shalt not catch the house on fire.

It goes without saying that gas and charcoal grills should never be used inside, right? Still, even the savviest of outdoor cooks has been known to make a bone-headed move or two. That's OK; we're only human. But before you get started, make sure of a few things:

- Situate the grill away from trees and shrubs, especially when it's extra dry outside. It's not a bad idea to keep a fire extinguisher on hand.

- Trim some fat. Some steaks, for example, come with an extra layer of fat, which you can easily cut away. Too much fat dripping into a fire can cause dangerous flare-ups. The same goes for heavy-handed saucing. For small flare-ups, move the meat out of the way of the flame and let it burn out.

- Grease fire? Hold the water, which can make it worse. Turn off the gas or close up the vents on a charcoal grill, if you can. A box of salt dumped on a grease fire can often extinguish it, if the fire's not too bad, but don't be afraid to call for help if it gets out of control.

2 Thou shalt not poison thy family.

Fire isn't the only hazard when grilling. There's also the matter of meat being kept at potentially dangerous temperatures. Starting from frozen is fine, but make sure meat is thoroughly thawed in the refrigerator before you attempt to cook it—this could take days, depending on the size and density of the meat. And, if you're cooking meat outside, keep it in the refrigerator until it's almost time to cook and then let it come up to room temperature. Leaving meat to sit in the sun while the grill gets up to temp is not a good idea.

3 Thou shalt keep thy work area clean.

Cross contamination can be a real problem. In our kitchen, we use color-coded cutting boards to keep meat separate from vegetables. Take a tip from the pros and cut raw meat on its own cutting board. Wash hands thoroughly and often. Nothing ruins a dinner like a bad case of food poisoning.

4 Thou shalt protect thy skin.

If you aren't a big fan of oven mitts (and many aren't), at least be sure to keep a number of kitchen towels on hand. Keep them dry and make sure to get into the habit of grabbing every single pan or tool you encounter with said towel, even if you know it's not hot. For every ten things you think are cool enough to grab in a kitchen, there's at least one that isn't. Why play Russian roulette with your fingers?

5 Thou shalt be prepared.

Mise en place. That's a fancy French term that means, "Get your act together." OK, literally it means, "setting in place," but the gist is to prepare the ingredients and building blocks you need to finish a dish, and put them in an accessible spot. That way, you're not running all over the place looking for missing ingredients while the rest of your recipe is burning (or even worse, on fire).

6 Thou shalt lubricate.

An oiled grill surface is your friend. Take a kitchen towel you won't be sad to see destroyed, soak up a little high smoke-point vegetable oil like canola, and carefully and thoroughly wipe down your preheated grill grates before adding the meat. Just don't use too much oil (see commandment No. 1).

7 Thou shalt properly season.

The only thing worse than under-seasoned meat is over-salted meat. Season well, but season judiciously. Remember that a piece of meat with a hefty amount of seasoning on the exterior will have essentially no seasoning in the center. It's all about balance.

8 Thou shalt be patient.

Will that piece of meat that you just now put on the grill not flip this very second? Stop touching it. Back away. Have a beer. It will move when it's ready. Seriously, stop.

9 Thou shalt be sure there is plenty of fuel.

This should go without saying, but nothing ruins a barbecue like running out of juice halfway through. Always make sure that if you're grilling over gas you've got a full tank. Real grill aficionados keep an extra tank on hand just in case. If you're grilling over charcoal, don't skimp; buy more than you think you'll need. As long as it's stored in a cool, dry place, charcoal keeps indefinitely. You'll use the extra eventually.

10 And, when it is over, thou shalt properly rest.

The meat, that is. When you cook meat, the muscle fibers contract in response to the high heat. Resting allows the fibers to relax and the juices to redistribute. Rest small cuts, like chops and steaks, for 5 minutes or so. Rest larger items, like whole chickens or the turkey on page 86, for longer. Chickens need about 15 minutes, while the turkey should rest for at least 20, but no more than 40.

II beef and pork

Though we do sauces and sides with panache, we'd be nothing without beef and pork. Our brisket would make a Texan barbecue master blush, but we suspect that it's the pork we make that keeps everyone coming back.

Food writer John Egerton called the noble and delicious pig "the sustainer of the South through four centuries of grief and glory." And though we have plenty of mud for wallowing and forage to be found, it's true that no pig around here is safe. Many proudly eat every part of the animal but the squeal: While the primal cuts are spirited away to market (or the smoker), the extra bits are fashioned into sausages, livermush, you name it.

Here at 12 Bones, we are known for our "tender butts and sweet racks." Ribs seem to be the first thing anyone ever orders—including presidents (see page 32 for more about that). It probably helps that we turn out some of the most unique bone-sucking sauces in the Southeast. Of course we'll share the secrets behind our funky pig polishes, which fold in ingredients like blueberries and Cheerwine along with more traditional fixings.

Don't fixate on the ribs to the exclusion of pulled pork though. Smoked just right, with a good bit of crisp bark mixing with fat, we think it's one of the sweetest joys life has to offer. While we'll certainly credit our kitchen staff with coaxing wonders out of the meat, the pig itself deserves at least some credit for the magic.

★ A WORD ON RUBS

Though marinades often seem the province of the home cook, rubs tend to get more attention in the world of the barbecue master. Why?

Rubs deliver a punch of flavor—quickly. We like the way a dry surface hits the grill grate with a sizzle. A rub also helps build up a nice, flavorful crust. Marinades, not so much (which isn't to say you can't, but we mostly prefer them for thinner cuts of meat, like a flank steak). We also do a lot of brining (see page 19 for more).

Though all the rubs in this chapter call for ground spices, we do recommend purchasing whole spices if you want to take your flavors to the next level. Buying pre-made rubs is perfectly fine, but creating your own is cheaper and allows for more experimentation.

To take it a step farther, try toasting whole spices. While toasting spices before grilling may seem a bit redundant, doing so helps release the oils within, which then permeate the meat as it cooks. This is particularly the case with cumin, which releases its warm, earthy aroma when toasted. Toasted coriander takes on a floral and nutty flavor that's muted when not toasted.

Here's how: Put the spices you're going to use for your recipe into a dry pan, preheated over medium heat, and shake the seeds around until they begin to brown lightly. You'll eventually learn to smell when they're done; spices release a deeper, toasty aroma when ready. Remove the pan from the heat and pour the spices onto a plate. They can go from perfectly toasted to scorched and bitter in a matter of seconds.

Next, it's time to break your spices down into smaller bits. You can use a spice or coffee grinder kept solely for the purpose. (Not ready to buy an extra grinder? See the pro tip that follows.) Or go old-fashioned and use a mortar and pestle. If you're the type who likes spices coarse enough for a flavorful crunch, à la steak au poivre, a mortar and pestle will deliver the right touch.

The process of seasoning meat with a spice rub is a simple one. In fact, it's right there in the name. First, pat your meat dry. Then, using a fair amount of pressure, liberally season the entire surface of the meat, rubbing the flavor into the crooks and crevices. Shake off any excess, and toss the seasoned meat onto your hot and well-lubricated surface (for grill tips, see page 16). For even better flavor penetration, set the meat aside and let the rub work its magic for at least an hour.

Dry rubs can be kept in an airtight container almost indefinitely, though they do tend to lose flavor over time.

A word of caution: Discard any spices that come in contact with raw meat. Keep your hands clean in order to avoid contaminating rubs.

Pro tip: Yes, you can use your coffee grinder to grind spices in a pinch. If some spice residue remains, clean it out with rice before your next batch of beans. Fill the grinder to the fill line with uncooked grains of rice, turn on the grinder, and let it whirl the grains around for about 30 seconds. The rice will absorb all of the extra flavors left over in the grinder. Dump the rice out into the garbage after use.

GARLIC RIB RUB

Yield: About 3½ cups. Use approximately 1 cup per rack of ribs.

10 ounces minced garlic
1½ cups vegetable oil
2 tablespoons kosher salt
2 tablespoons dried ginger

2 tablespoons red pepper flakes
2 tablespoons dried basil
2 tablespoons dried oregano

Combine all the ingredients and mix thoroughly. Store what isn't used in an airtight container and refrigerate.

12 BONES CHICKEN RUB

This makes enough for several batches of chicken. We also use it to season our smoked shrimp and other recipes. This chicken rub is a good all-purpose rub, something that can be used in multiple applications.

½ cup paprika
½ cup granulated garlic
¼ cup granulated onion
½ cup fine-ground black pepper
1 tablespoon cayenne
4 teaspoons whole dry basil
1 tablespoon cumin

4 teaspoons dark brown sugar
¼ cup Old Bay seasoning
4 teaspoons dried sage
¼ cup dry English mustard
½ cup iodized salt
8 teaspoons chili powder

Combine all ingredients and mix thoroughly. Store what isn't used in an airtight container and refrigerate.

SEASONING SALT

This is a great all-purpose seasoning salt that's excellent for flavoring fried chicken, wings, ribs, or any other recipe that calls for it. It's a wonderful alternative to similar items you'll find in the store, many of which come packed full of MSG and preservatives. Put this together once, keep it cool and dry, and you'll find you have a convenient jar of flavor-enhancer at your fingertips.

Yield: 3 cups

10 ounces iodized salt
1 cup sugar
¼ cup paprika
½ tablespoon celery salt

½ tablespoon granulated garlic
½ tablespoon granulated onion
½ tablespoon dry English mustard

Whisk together all ingredients and store in an airtight container.

12 BONES BUTT RUB

This is what we use on our big Boston butts—which eventually become pulled pork—before smoking. You can do the same (see recipes for Pork Butt on pages 34 and 37), or you can use it on a regular, oven-roasted pork loin, if you want. This has a rather earthy flavor, which separates it from many store-bought rubs you'll find. It may seem full-flavored at first glance since pork has a neutral flavor, but the fat can easily drown out spices if you go too light.

Yield: 4½ cups
1 cup iodized salt
¼ cup cayenne
2 cups paprika
½ cup granulated garlic
1½ tablespoons dry
    English mustard
2½ tablespoons dry
    whole oregano
2½ tablespoons seasoning
    salt (store-bought, or use the
    recipe on page 26)
2½ tablespoons fine ground
    black pepper
1 tablespoon cumin
1 tablespoon ground nutmeg
1 tablespoon cinnamon
1 tablespoon ground allspice

Combine all the ingredients and mix thoroughly. Store what isn't used in an airtight container.

SALT-AND-PEPPER "NEKKID" BABY BACK RIBS

Our customers love these ribs for their simplicity; nothing interferes with the flavor of smoke, time, and perfectly cooked pork. As barbecue aficionados know, unadorned meat is the best yardstick by which to measure a 'cue joint's worth. Without the benefit of a drape of sweet sauce here or sash of pepper vinegar there, there's just nowhere for a sub-par rib to hide.

That's the idea behind this recipe. Treat these ribs as a straightforward boast of your own grill prowess. Or use a rack as a blank canvas—the variations are practically endless. Though few would begrudge a plate of simple, hot, and smoky ribs, a splash of sticky sauce still makes these ribs sing (and a giant mess, for that matter).

If you like it sweet, check out the recipe for our favorite workhorse sauce, the 12 Bones Tomato "Q," which kicks off all of the sauce recipes on page 102. You can use that sauce as a base on which to build other favorites—take the Blueberry-Chipotle Barbecue Sauce, which won *Good Morning America*'s Best Bite Contest. Spice hounds can turn to page 118 to see our recipe for Jalapeño "Q" Sauce. (And don't forget the paper towels.) Plan to serve about four ribs per person. (Typically, more than one rack is made if you're cooking for a crowd.)

Sprinkle salt and pepper evenly on the ribs. Smoke them at 260 to 275°F (and no higher than 280°F) for 3 to 3½ hours, or until rib bones pull loose from the meat. (For complete smoking instructions, see page 13.) Baste the ribs with Mop Sauce (recipe and method on page 105) after the first hour of cooking, then every half hour thereafter.

After 3 hours, check the ribs to see if they're done. You can tell when the ribs are done when the meat easily pulls away from the bone.

If you want to add some extra char to the ribs, finish them over medium-high heat on the grill, and brush them with the barbecue sauce of your choice before serving.

Yield: 1 rack, about 12–13 bones.

- 1 rack baby back ribs, skinless (Note: When raw, one rack of our ribs weighs between 2 and 2½ pounds.)
- 2 tablespoons kosher salt
- 1 teaspoon coarse-ground black pepper
- 12 Bones Mop Sauce (page 105)

ingredient spotlight:
BABY BACK
RIBS

What are baby back ribs? And why are they called that?

It's easy to get befuddled when it comes to different cuts of meat. Pigs have spareribs, while the same cut on a cow is called a short rib. A pork butt is actually located near the shoulder, while the tenderloin is found near the spine. Among the different types of pork ribs are baby backs and baby spareribs, neither of which has anything to do with the age of the animal.

Even baby back ribs have enough names to confuse the sharpest of shoppers. You may find baby back ribs labeled as any of the following things in your meat aisle: loin back ribs, back ribs, loin ribs, baby backs, even Canadian backs.

We like baby backs because their lower fat and meat content make them quicker to cook. For that matter, they're a bit more compact and easier to eat than a sparerib, which would be perfectly at home on Fred Flintstone's dinner plate.

When purchasing ribs, it's important to remember that you can expect one person to eat, at the very least, about four ribs. We've known plenty who can polish off a full rack—that's about 12 bones, in case you were wondering.

BROWN SUGAR BABY BACK RIBS

Yield: 1 rack of baby back ribs (note: when raw one of our racks weighs between 2-2.5 lbs)

Approx. 1 cup of 12 Bones brown sugar rub

Use approximately 1 handful of rub per rack of ribs.

For the rub:

1   pound dark brown sugar

¾ cup 12 Bones Chicken Rub (page 26)

These ribs are fit for a king—or at least a U.S. president.

The sweet, brown sugar dry rub melts as the ribs are cooked, which forms a nice crust. They're great dry, but the 12 Bones Tomato "Q" Sauce (page 102) would work just fine if you want to add a little extra something. By the time these get to the table, they'll be pretty gooey. If you're a spice fan, try a few shakes of hot sauce.

Lay rack on large platter or baking pan large enough for ribs to fit without hanging over the edges. Pat dry excess moisture with paper towels. If the surface of the ribs is too wet the rub will end up on the bottom of your smoker instead of on your ribs. Spread rub evenly over meat side of ribs with your hands and press into meat to form crust. Smoke at 260 to 275 degrees for 2½ to 3 hours. (For complete smoking instructions see page 13.) After 2½ hours check for doneness by twisting one of the ribs in the center of the rack with tongs. Bone should twist slightly. If you like your ribs falling off the bone, continue to cook to desired tenderness. (Be careful not to overcook, ribs will go from tender and moist to dry and grainy.)

customer spotlight:
PRESIDENT
OBAMA

While we love Brown Sugar Baby Back Ribs for their simplicity and the fact that the rub creates a beautiful crust on the grill, we also happen to know that this is the version President Obama prefers.

The first time President Obama dropped by the restaurant was in 2008, while he was touring the country in support of his campaign to snag the job as commander in chief. These ribs were also on his agenda.

According to a White House statement released after President Obama was elected, he liked it here in Asheville so much that he vowed to return with his family. Not only did he make good on his promise in 2010, he returned to 12 Bones so quickly that it made the collective heads of our local press spin. Barely had Air Force One touched wheels to tarmac when the presidential motorcade gunned it for our tiny restaurant. His visit was not without fanfare.

"The second time was a little more impressive in my eyes," says Tom Montgomery, who owned the restaurant at the time of the visit. "He was president at that point, and we had helicopters overhead, guys on the rooftops with sniper rifles, and Secret Service guys at each door."

Tom and Sabra weren't even in the restaurant at the time, because they were busy opening our second location on the south side of Asheville. "One of the employees called us and said they had shown up with three SUVs," recalls Tom. "And lots of men with guns."

But even if the presidential motorcade took nearly everyone in Asheville by surprise in heading straight to 12 Bones from the airport, Tom had a suspicion President Obama would show up sooner or later, he says.

"We had an idea earlier in the week because we kept having a group of four black suits come in and eat lunch," he says. "One day, one of the guys paid with a White House Credit Union credit card, which actually had a picture of the White House on it."

In 2010, President Obama also ordered up the Brown Sugar Baby Back Ribs, which were prepared, plated, and served under the watchful eye of the Secret Service, who were charged with ensuring no foul play befell the president's plate. But even with all of the surveillance, Tom reports that the day was actually a piece of cake.

"It was surprisingly easy, because he was so down to earth," Tom remembers. President Obama joked with the staff, said he loved his ribs, and even insisted on getting a picture with the crew.

The third time he came through was in 2013. During a speech at a local factory, President Obama said that there are two things that keep him coming back to our mountain city. "Number one is, I really like the people," he said. "And number two is 12 Bones, which I will be stopping by on the way back to the airport."

SMOKIN' HOT PORK BUTT

When it comes to barbecue, there's an ongoing debate about what truly authentic 'cue really is. In North Carolina, that debate borders on an all-out squabble. In the eastern part of the state, you'll find many who swear that whole hog is the only way to go. Farther out west, particularly in our neck of the woods, we tend to go for big old hunks of meat from the shoulder.

It seems like the only thing most factions can agree on is that true barbecue is laced with the flavor of a long, slow roast over hardwood. That's why some may take issue with this recipe, which calls for smoking the meat only halfway, and then finishing it in the oven.

For those with a desire to stand outside all day and baste to their heart's content, skip the oven and keep smoking until your pork butt and all of its connective tissue and fat have slumped and melted to form the heavenly mess that is perfect barbecue. Look for an internal temperature between 190 and 205°F, and you're done.

This recipe is for those who can't, or don't want to, stay outside all day. Using boneless pork butt and finishing it in the oven means you're saving time, not only on the day of, but also the days beforehand.

That's because no brining is necessary for this pork butt to turn out plenty moist. And, since the cut is boneless, there will be more nooks and crannies to get the rub inside, which will give it plenty of flavor. Bring this dish to a potluck or summer picnic and you'll be the king of the neighborhood. If you want to pretend you worked at it for 12 hours, we won't tell anyone.

Mix the Butt Rub in just enough water (about ¼ cup) to make a thick paste.

Thoroughly coat the pork butt, making sure to get the seasoning in all the crevices. Soak the wood chips and prepare a grill or smoker for indirect heat between 225 and 240°F, but no higher than 240°F (see page 13 for more tips on smoking). Smoke the pork butt over indirect heat for 3 to 4 hours, or until a good, dark crust forms. The internal temperature should reach about 170°F.

Meanwhile, preheat the oven to 300°F. Transfer the pork butt to a roasting pan. Chef Shane says he likes to line the bottom of the pan with some onions and garlic, on top of which he sets the pork butt, which keeps it from sitting in its own fat. Cover the pan with foil, tenting the foil to make sure it doesn't touch the butt. Finish in the oven until the internal temperature reaches 190 to 205°F, which should take about 4 hours.

Let the butt rest for about 30 minutes, then slice, pull, or chop it. Serve with the "Q" sauce of your choice or plain.

Yield: 8–10 servings

- 1 (5–6 pound) boneless pork butt
- ¾ cup 12 Bones Butt Rub (page 27)

OVEN-ROASTED PULLED PORK BUTT

Yield: 8 servings

1 (4–5 pound) boneless pork butt

½ cup 12 Bones Chicken Rub (page 26)

2 large onions, sliced ¼-inch thick

10 cloves fresh garlic, peeled

If you're not in the grilling mood, or if it's too cold outside to man the smoker, this is the recipe for you: tender, fall-off-the-bone pork, made extra succulent with the addition of the cooking juices at the end. Pair this pork with rolls and a sauce of your choice (recipes start on page 100) for an indoor picnic come January. To make this pork butt taste even more like it belongs at a summer barbecue, mix the drippings with an equal amount of your choice of barbecue sauce. Then mix that liquid with the pulled pork.

In a medium-size mixing bowl, rub the pork butt with the 12 Bones Chicken Rub, being sure to get the seasonings into all the crevices. Cover the bowl and chill overnight, or for at least 2 hours. Preheat the oven to 425°F. Line a roasting pan with heavy-duty aluminum foil. Layer the onion slices and the garlic in the bottom of the pan (over the foil, of course). Place the pork, fat-side up, on top of the veggies, and then place the roasting pan in the preheated oven. Roast for 30 minutes, uncovered.

After the 30 minutes is up, remove the pan and tent some foil over the pork. Place the pork back in the oven and reduce the temperature to 275°F. Cook for 4 hours, or until tender. Remove the pork from the oven, remove the foil tent, and allow the pork to rest for 20 minutes in the pan. Then, remove the pork from the roasting pan and strain out the drippings and reserve. Skim the fat from the drippings, and once the pork is cool enough to handle, pull it. Pour the drippings over the pulled pork and serve.

 # SMOKED BEEF BRISKET

We only use a dry rub on this Texas-style brisket. That's because we smoke our briskets right beneath our pork loins, an arrangement that means sweet, smoky pork fat saturates the beef while it's cooking, creating a natural sauce. We don't expect you'll be doing the same thing at home, so we recommend adding Mop Sauce for some additional moisture.

We use Angus beef and suggest you use the same or another high-quality beef brisket. Serve this brisket sliced, on a bun with your choice of barbecue sauce. To make chopped brisket, mix the chopped meat with ¾ cup of 12 Bones Tomato "Q" Sauce, or other sweet barbecue sauce, per pound.

Yield: 6–8 servings

- 1 flat cut brisket (6–7 pounds average)
- ⅔ cup 12 Bones Chicken Rub (page 26)
- 1 cup 12 Bones Mop Sauce (page 105)

Liberally sprinkle the brisket with the 12 Bones Chicken Rub. Massage the rub thoroughly into the meat, covering crevices and all surfaces. Chill the brisket, uncovered, for about 30 minutes to an hour. Meanwhile, soak the wood chips and prepare the grill or smoker for indirect heat at 225 to 235°F. Use cherry wood chips for this job. See page 13 for smoking tips.

Place the brisket on the unfired side, and then close the lid. The temperature of the smoker should not go below 220°F or exceed 240°F during the cooking process (smoke for one hour, adding more wood and coals as needed). Baste the brisket with Mop Sauce and flip it over, then baste the other side, and close the lid. Baste and flip every hour or so, until brisket reaches an internal temperature between 195 and 205°F. This should take about 6 hours.

Once it's ready, remove the brisket from the smoker and allow it to rest at room temperature for about 15 minutes. Slice the meat against the grain in thin slices, and only slice what you are planning to serve. Wrap the leftover brisket and store it in the refrigerator. Reheat with Mop Sauce, use leftovers for Brunswick Stew (page 188), or pile it on bread to make a big, bad sandwich.

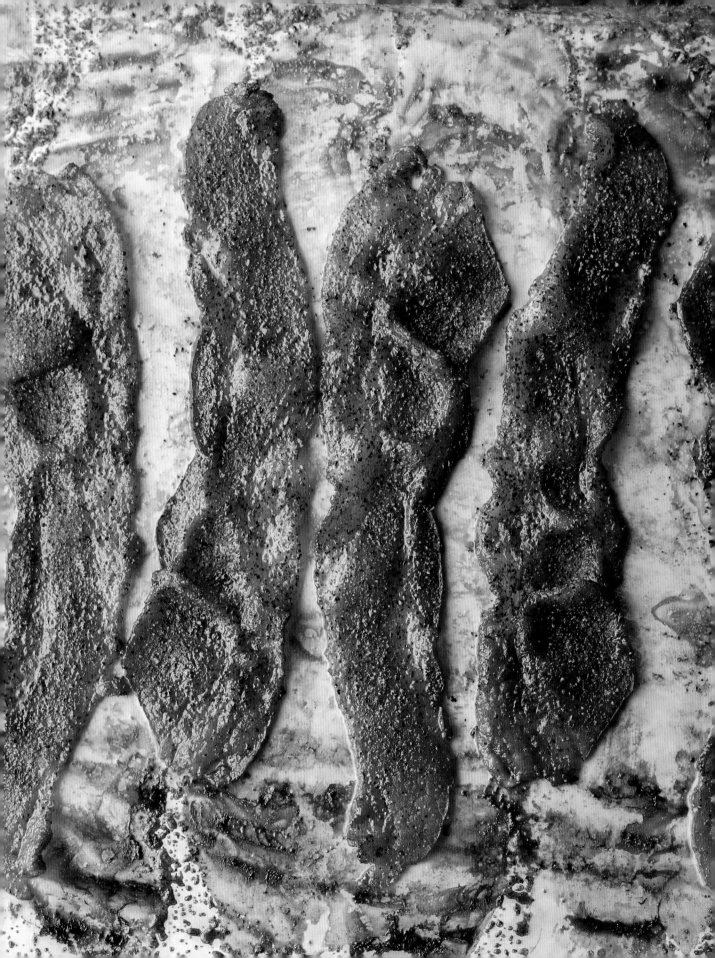

BROWN SUGAR BACON

Yield: 6–8 servings

For the 12 Bones Bacon Sugar:

½ cup dark brown sugar

2 tablespoons fine-ground black pepper

1½ teaspoons chili powder

1 teaspoon cayenne pepper

For the bacon:

8 ounces sliced bacon (about eight pieces, enough for two sandwiches)

8 teaspoons 12 Bones Bacon Sugar

We think this sweet and peppery bacon recipe makes everything taste better. However, our customers' favorite way to eat it is in the ultimate BLT. We stack our BLTs with fried green tomatoes (page 148) so we can serve a good sandwich year-round, even when tomatoes aren't in season. We also like the acidity of green tomatoes, and we kick the tomato flavor up a notch with a generous smear of Sun-dried Tomato Pesto Mayo (see the recipe on page 91).

Note: If properly dried, the sugar mix for this recipe will keep almost indefinitely, and you can bring it out any time you need to whip up a batch of bacon.

Thoroughly combine the sugar, pepper, chili powder, and cayenne in a small mixing bowl. Once combined, spread the mixture evenly on a microwave-safe plate. Microwave the sugar mixture on high for 20 seconds, then repeat the process until the mixture feels completely dry. It should take about ten 20-second intervals. Once the mixture is completely dry, grind it into a fine powder in a food processor or spice grinder. Store in an airtight container.

Preheat the oven to 400°F. Line a cookie sheet with a nonstick silicon mat or parchment paper. Arrange the bacon on a single layer on the cookie sheet and sprinkle each piece with one teaspoon of the Bacon Sugar. Bake for 15 minutes, rotating the pan halfway through the cooking process.

Allow to cool for 5 minutes before serving.

a word on:
SAUSAGE

Sausage is a beautiful thing. The ancient Greeks knew it. Homer even wrote about sausage in the *Odyssey*: "There are some goats' paunches down at the fire, which we have filled with blood and fat, and set aside for supper; he who is victorious and proves himself to be the better man shall have his pick of the lot."

In modern times, an electric grinder is incredibly helpful for making sausage. If you plan to get into the sausage-making craft, we highly recommend you look into purchasing one. All the recipes we've included in this book for making sausage assume you're using a grinder.

If you don't have a grinder, there are only a few recipes to skip. Might we suggest the meatloaf (page 73) instead? If you do have a grinder, you're almost ready to get going. Here are a few other things to keep in mind.

Keep it cold: Aside from the obvious issues of food safety (bacteria begins to multiply rapidly at 40°F), keeping your meat—and equipment—freezing cold is crucial to good sausage. When fat gets too warm, it "smears," which can cause textural issues. It can leave pockets of broken-down fat, and pools of fat are as unsavory as they sound.

The case for casing: If you decide to make sausage links, you'll want to purchase a sausage stuffer. Sausage stuffers can get pricey, but they're a worthy investment if you plan to make sausage-making a habit. Ask your butcher for natural casings, which are made from parts of, typically, cow, pig, or lamb intestine. Natural casings require repeated rinses to flush them of salt and impurities.

You can keep unused casings for a few days covered in salt. You can also find synthetic casings, some of which are edible (and some of which are not). If you're going the synthetic route, we recommend collagen casings, if you can find them.

If you skip the casing: You may decide to settle for free-form sausages too. Simply shape them by hand into patties and, when you're ready to cook them, brown them in a frying pan. Or bake ½-inch thick, 3 to 4 ounce patties in a 300°F oven on a foil-covered cookie sheet until they reach an internal temperature of 165°F. This should take about 15 to 20 minutes.

If you decide to make links: Smoke links over indirect heat, between 180 and 200°F, until they reach an internal temperature of 140°F. That should take about 20 minutes. Let links rest for at least 15 minutes and up to 30 minutes. Then grill them over direct heat to brown the outside of the sausage and serve.

SMOKEHOUSE BRATWURST

We go through most of our bratwurst in the famous Hogzilla sandwich (see 46). However, you don't have to limit this recipe's use to a giant tower of pork between two buns. These brats are great on their own, right off the grill, with a touch of mustard.

Since they are emulsified, they hold up to a double-cooking process quite well. That also makes them great for tailgating—smoke the brats ahead of time and then finish them on the grill any old time you want. They're unlikely to dry out if you've done everything the right way.

Equipment:
Stand-up mixer with grinder attachment and paddle.

Grinding blade with large die.

Sausage stuffer, only if you're going to work the ground meat into casings. Ask your local butcher for hog casings if you're planning to make links.

Yield: 6–8 servings
1 pound boneless pork butt, cut into 1-inch cubes, kept cold
1 teaspoon kosher salt
½ teaspoon ground black pepper
½ teaspoon ground ginger
¼ teaspoon ground nutmeg
¼ cup heavy cream, kept cold
1 egg, also kept cold

Toss the pork cubes with salt, pepper, ginger, and nutmeg. Once mixed, chill the pork in the freezer, along with the grinder parts, for about 15 minutes. Meanwhile, chill the mixing bowl and the paddle in the fridge. Assemble the grinder to the manufacturer's instructions. The faster you work, the better. All the parts need to stay as cold as possible throughout this process.

Once properly chilled, grind the meat on high speed, directly into your chilled mixing bowl. Remove the grinder attachment. Mix your newly ground sausage in the stand-up mixer with the chilled paddle attachment on medium speed. With the mixer running drizzle in the cream slowly. Add the egg, and mix with the paddle for 1 minute. Stop the machine and scrape the bowl and paddle. Then, continue to mix until the meat begins to stick to the sides of the bowl. This should take about 2 minutes. Pat a piece of plastic wrap directly on top of the meat in the bowl, or transfer the meat to an airtight container and chill. Sanitize all parts of the machine. See page 43 for cooking instructions.

HOGZILLA

Hogzilla was named after a wild and domestic pig hybrid, which was captured in Georgia and weighed more than 1,000 pounds. Hogzilla, the sandwich, is apparently equally as captivating, and the Travel Channel Network filmed the crew building the thing for an episode of *Sandwich Paradise*. The sandwich, created by one of our founding partners, Ron Brannon, contains one 6-inch link of our Smokehouse Bratwurst, plus pulled pork and 12 Bones Brown Sugar Bacon (page 41).

We'd like to tell you not to try this at home, but here's the recipe (per sandwich), just in case:

    6-inch hoagie roll

    Butter

    1 Smokehouse Bratwurst link, butterflied

    4 ounces of pulled pork

    2 pieces of 12 Bones Brown Sugar Bacon

    2 slices pepper jack cheese

Butter the inside of a 16-inch hoagie roll, and then toast it under a broiler. Remove the roll from the oven, and lay the bratwurst on the bottom piece, cut side up. Then add the pork, the bacon, and finally, the pepper jack cheese. Then place it back under the broiler until the cheese is melted. Replace the top of the roll, and you have yourself a Hogzilla.

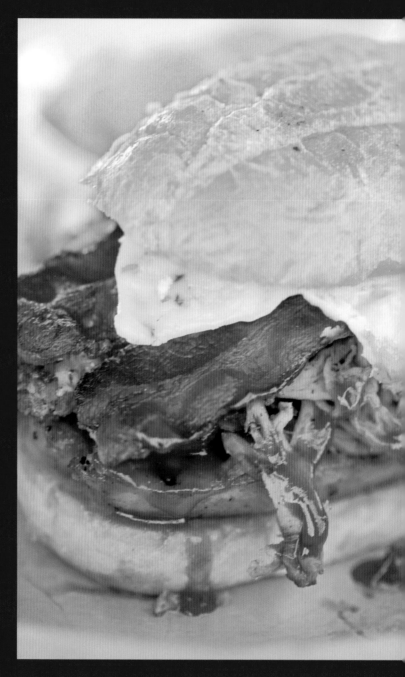

HOUSE SAUSAGE

Yield: 6–8 servings

1   pound pork butt with fat,
    cut into 1-inch chunks

1   teaspoon kosher salt

1   tablespoon
    onion powder

1   teaspoon whole
    fennel seeds

1   teaspoon red
    pepper flakes

This is a very traditional sausage, the type you might like to eat for breakfast with a mess of eggs and toast. At 12 Bones, we don't serve breakfast. Still, we think it's worth our time to make our own sausage since we use it to build flavor in a variety of our rotating sides, including favorites like Black-eyed Peas with Jalapeños, Cornbread Stuffing, and Mushroom Casserole. We also use it in the occasional special, like the Cabbage Sausage Rolls recipe that follows this one.

Equipment:
Stand-up mixer with grinder attachment and paddle.

Grinding blade with small die.

In a medium mixing bowl, combine all the ingredients. Cover the bowl and place it in the freezer, along with the grinder attachment of the stand-up mixer, for 20 minutes. Chill an additional mixing bowl in the fridge. Assemble the grinder to the manufacturer's instructions. Working quickly, grind the cold meat directly into the cold mixing bowl. Run the ground meat through the grinder a second time and chill the sausage for at least 15 minutes in the fridge before using. See page 42 for cooking instructions and sausage-making tips, or use in the following recipe.

> **Note:** Meat can be stored in a freezer bag. Squeeze out as much air as possible before sealing the bag and freeze.

CABBAGE
SAUSAGE ROLLS

We don't often find ourselves with extra sausage around the restaurant. However, in the rare times we do, we think it's one of the best "problems" to have. While it's not a classic barbecue dish, these cabbage rolls are one of our favorite off-the-cuff creations to make use of a couple pounds of sausage. Collard green leaves work just as well, but they're larger so they'll need even more meat, or you'll yield fewer rolls.

Place one cabbage leaf on a flat surface, such as a cutting board. Using a rolling pin, roll over the leaf to flatten the veins. Repeat with the remaining leaves, and then set aside. Combine the sausage, egg, and rice in a mixing bowl, and mix thoroughly with your hands. Lay one leaf on a work surface, and place one-eighth of the meat mixture—about 4 ounces—in the center of the leaf. Shape into a little meat log, so that there is 1 inch of space between the edge of the log and each leaf. Fold in the sides of the leaf over the meat filling. Starting at an unfolded edge, roll up the leaf to completely enclose the filling. Place the roll, seam side down, on a baking sheet. Repeat this process with the remaining leaves. Chill, uncovered, in the refrigerator while making the sauce.

To make the sauce, toast the fennel seeds over medium heat in a 12-inch skillet, moving the pan occasionally until the seeds are fragrant. Do not burn. Remove the seeds from the pan and set aside, and then add just enough olive oil to coat the pan. Add the garlic and the shallot, and stir over medium heat until they're soft but not browned. Stir in the wine, and then reduce until the pan is almost dry. Stir in the tomato sauce, bring to a boil, and then reduce the heat to low. Crush the fennel seeds, then add them to the sauce. Simmer for about 15 minutes, and season with salt and pepper. Remove sauce from heat and preheat oven to 375°. Add half the sauce to a 9 x 13-inch casserole dish. Place the cabbage rolls on top of the sauce. Pour the rest of the sauce over the rolls. Place a piece of wax paper or parchment on top, and then cover with foil. Bake in the center of the oven at 375°F for 30 minutes. Carefully remove the foil and paper, and bake for another 20 minutes. Check the internal temperature: Serve at 150°F.

Yield: 8 servings

For the rolls:

8   large cabbage leaves

2   pounds uncooked, uncased 12 Bones House Sausage (page 47)

1   large egg

1   cup cooked, long-grain rice

For the sauce:

1   teaspoon whole fennel seeds

Olive oil

¼   cup 12 Bones Roasted Garlic (page 55)

1   large shallot, minced

1   cup dry white wine

4   cups canned tomato sauce

  Salt and pepper to taste

ANDOUILLE

Yield: About 12 servings

- 4 pounds pork butt
- 1 pound fatback, fresh, skinless, and unsalted
- 4 tablespoons paprika
- 1 tablespoon black pepper
- 1 tablespoon cumin
- 1 tablespoon cayenne
- 1 tablespoon salt
- 1 teaspoon red pepper flakes
- 1 teaspoon oregano
- 1 teaspoon thyme
- 1 teaspoon coriander
- ¼ cup onion powder
- ¼ cup garlic, (smoked, sautéed, or oven roasted)

Andouille is most often associated with Cajun cooking. It's a star player in gumbo and makes red beans and rice sing. This is a slightly spicy sausage, and it has an aggressive flavor that will stand up to just about anything you add it to. At 12 Bones, we grill this up and pile it on a hoagie roll with sautéed peppers and onions, then smother it with melted cheese. It's also a great substitute sausage for dishes where you want to punch up the heat.

First, cube the pork into approximately 1-inch pieces. Then, combine all the remaining ingredients except the garlic with the pork and chill for at least a few hours, or up to 24 hours, to allow the spices to permeate the meat. Next, rough chop the garlic. Cover, and set aside.

Using a medium die, grind all the pork into a chilled bowl. In a separate bowl combine half of the meat with the garlic. Grind the other half of the meat with a small die. This method gives you some chunkier meat and garlic pieces, with the meat ground on the small die acting as the binding agent. Work quickly so that meat stays cold and does not smear (see page 42 for more about that).

Now, combine everything and mix well. Stuff in medium hog casings, or shape as needed. Smoke or cook in the oven at 275°F for 2 hours, or until the internal temperature reaches 150°F, (if you plan to cook it on a grill or in another dish later). If you plan to eat right away, cook to 165°F.

JAMAICAN JERK
GRILLED PORK LOIN

This is one of the few meats that we grill rather than smoke because we like the way the high heat chars the rub and gives it a blackened flavor. The ways to serve it are numerous. You could slice this pork thin and layer it with pickles and Swiss cheese to make an amazing Cuban sandwich (one of our fastest-selling specials). Or, slice it thick and serve it with our White Cheddar Spuds on page 183. The end pieces are also excellent tossed into soups and chowders.

Since brining a pork loin really takes it over the top, we recommend spending the extra 24 hours to do so—so be sure to plan accordingly. If you skip this step, the result will not be quite as juicy.

Place the loin in a nonreactive container, large enough to allow a 2- to 4-inch space around and above the loin (you can cut the loin in half if you need to) and refrigerate. In a 4- to 6-quart saucepan, whisk together water, salt, ¼ cup of the jerk rub, sugar, coriander, peppercorns, cinnamon stick, and ginger to create the flavoring brine for the pork. Simmer this mixture over low heat for about 30 minutes, stirring to dissolve the sugar and salt. Next, remove the brine from the heat, cover the pot, and steep for about 30 minutes to let the flavors develop. Add the ice, and pour the now-chilled brine over the loin. Cover and chill for at least 24 hours.

Remove the pork loin from the brine, and wipe the coriander and peppercorns off the loin. Your brine has done its work, so you'll need to discard it. No, you can't use it again. Pat the loin dry with a clean towel. Season with remaining ½ cup of jerk seasoning and refrigerate, uncovered, for 1 hour.

Meanwhile, light the grill or the coals and bring the temperature up to 400 to 425°F. Grill your loin over direct heat with the lid of the grill open, rolling it around to brown the outside, and then close the lid. If you're using a gas grill, reduce the heat to 350°F. If using coals, just close the lid and vents. Cook until the internal temperature of the meat reaches 155°F in the thickest part of the loin, or until the juices run clear. Rest the meat at room temperature for 30 to 40 minutes before slicing.

Yield: 6–8 servings

1	boneless, center-cut pork loin, 4–6 pounds
2	quarts water
½	cup kosher salt
¾	cup Jamaican Jerk Seasoning (recipe follows—use more or less, depending on the size of the loin)
½	cup packed brown sugar
1	tablespoon whole coriander seed
1	tablespoon black peppercorns
1	cinnamon stick
2	ounces ginger root, peeled and rough chopped (see page 66 for a Pro tip on peeling ginger)
2	pounds of ice

JAMAICAN JERK SEASONING

This flavorful rub is great on chicken, pork, and fish. You'll need a bit less than a cup for the Jamaican Jerk Pork Loin in the preceding recipe, so make sure to stow away what you don't use in your spice cabinet for the next time you need it. We bet it won't stick around for long.

Yield: 2 cups, enough for two pork loins, and then some

½ cup dark brown sugar
2 tablespoons iodized salt
2 tablespoons granulated garlic
2 tablespoons granulated onion
2 tablespoons dried thyme
1 tablespoon ground cumin
2 teaspoons ground cinnamon
2 teaspoons ground nutmeg
2 teaspoons ground coriander
2 teaspoons cayenne
½ teaspoon ground ginger
½ teaspoon ground allspice
½ teaspoon ground cloves

Thoroughly whisk together all the ingredients so that there are no lumps remaining. Store in an airtight container.

BEER-BRAISED PORK CHEEKS

Here in Asheville, there's no shortage of good, dark, local craft beer. So when we have pork cheeks around, we grab some beer from the tap and start braising. The result is one of our rarest, but also tastiest, specials.

This recipe in particular was inspired by Chef Shane's stint on a Louisiana oil supply boat. The captain of that boat made a similar recipe by simmering chuck roast in beer, which he then served over rice with poblano peppers, celery, onions, and garlic. He never would show Shane exactly how to make it. The way Shane tells it, it's because he was from the wrong part of the South—which was anywhere but Louisiana. This is an attempt to re-create that jealously guarded recipe but with a smokehouse twist.

We love that cheeks don't have a lot of fat, though they do have a lot of collagen, which translates to a luscious dish with a sauce that requires minimal skimming while you cook. As the collagen cooks out of the cheeks, it thickens the sauce naturally—no need to make a roux or get cornstarch involved. Note that this is one of our recipes that requires a lot of marinating time, so plan accordingly. The cooking time is also quite long—but we think it's worth it. If you can't find cheeks, you may substitute pork shoulder or pork belly. The latter has the most fat.

With a sharp knife, score the fat side of each cheek four times at the same angle. Try to just slice through the fat layer and membrane, but not into the meat. Place the cheeks in a nonreactive container, such as a casserole dish or a mixing bowl. Cover the cheeks with the beer and garlic, and toss to coat them thoroughly. Cover the dish or bowl with plastic wrap and chill overnight. Marinate for at least 12 hours, and up to 48 hours. Remove the cheeks from the marinade, making sure to reserve the marinade.

Yield: 4–6 servings

2	pounds pork cheeks, trimmed of surrounding cartilage
4	cups of dark, bitter beer
½	cup 12 Bones Roasted Garlic (recipe follows), or substitute regular garlic
1	cup 12 Bones Tomato "Q" Sauce (page 102)
1	(14.5-ounce) can of fire-roasted diced tomatoes with juice
2	teaspoons kosher salt, plus more for seasoning,
1	teaspoon ground white pepper, plus more for seasoning
4	poblano peppers, stems and seeds removed, remaining flesh julienned
2	large yellow onions, julienned

Transfer the marinade to a 3- to 4- quart nonreactive saucepan. Bring it to a boil over medium-high heat, then reduce the heat to low and skim off the foam. Don't freak out, this is just protein released from the cheeks during the marinating process. Then, stir in the 12 Bones Tomato "Q" sauce, the tomatoes, 2 teaspoons of the salt, and 1 teaspoon of the white pepper. Remove this sauce from the heat and set aside.

Prepare a grill or smoker for indirect heat by pushing lit coals to one side or only turning on one side of your gas grill (see page 13 for a more thorough smoking explanation). Soak some applewood chips in room-temperature water for at least 30 minutes before adding to smoker.

Pat the cheeks dry with a clean towel and season liberally with salt and white pepper. Smoke the cheeks at a temperature between 250 and 275°F, until they are dark in color and a crust has just started to develop. This should take about 30 minutes.

Preheat the oven to 325°F. Layer the poblanos and the onions in the bottom of a roasting pan. Layer the cheeks, fat side up, on top of the veggies. Pour the sauce over the cheeks. Cover the roasting pan with aluminum foil and braise the cheeks in the preheated oven until they are spoon-tender, about 2 hours. Remove the roasting pan from the oven and skim off any fat floating on the top, which shouldn't be too much. Taste the sauce and adjust the seasonings as necessary.

12 BONES ROASTED GARLIC

<u>Yield: 4 cups</u>

2 cups whole, peeled garlic cloves
1 small yellow onion, diced
1 cup vegetable oil
2 teaspoons ground cumin
1 teaspoon dried oregano

1 teaspoon poultry seasoning
1 teaspoon kosher salt
½ teaspoon ground nutmeg
Pinch of ground cinnamon

Preheat oven to 300°F. Stir together all ingredients in an oven-safe pan. Cover and cook for 45 minutes. Store in airtight container and refrigerate for up to two weeks.

FLAT IRON
PASTRAMI

We love flat iron steaks, and we also dig the fact that they're becoming more popular and thus easier to find. Plus, they're great medium-rare, which we think is the best way to serve this pastrami. (Because of its low-fat content, we highly recommend you don't cook it past medium, or 160°F.) You can find flat iron steaks at your butcher or well-stocked grocery store. You may find that they're sometimes marked as "top blade."

We layer Flat Iron Pastrami on a sandwich with Dijon mustard and vinegar coleslaw. But for a perfect summer appetizer (or meal unto itself), try constructing a cold meat board with thinly sliced and chilled pastrami, pickled vegetables (see pages 151 to 163 for pickle recipes), and a dollop of mayonnaise or sour cream stirred with horseradish. Leftover pastrami also makes a great breakfast hash with home fries, poblanos, garlic, and onions.

Yield: 4 servings, with some for leftovers

1	flat iron steak, approximately 2 pounds
½	recipe 12 Bones Pastrami Brine (recipe follows)
1	tablespoon whole black peppercorns
1	tablespoon whole mustard seeds
1	tablespoon whole coriander

Place the steak in a glass or a plastic container, large and deep enough to hold both the meat and the brine, at least a 9 x 13-inch casserole dish. Stir the chilled pastrami brine and pour it over the steak. Flip the steak over and cover it, then set it in the refrigerator to chill for about 12 to 24 hours per pound.

Add the peppercorns, mustard seeds, and coriander to a small sauté pan. Heat the seeds over medium-high heat while moving the pan back and forth to keep them from scorching. Once the seeds are fragrant, about 5 minutes, pour them onto a plate and let them cool to room temperature. Once the seeds have cooled, grind them in a spice grinder or mortar and pestle.

Once the steak is through brining, remove it from the brining liquid and wipe off the spices. Pat the meat dry with a clean towel. Discard the brine at this point. Press your toasted spices into the surface of the meat, on both sides, and then chill the steak, uncovered.

Meanwhile, preheat your grill for direct heat, 400 to 425°F. Once the grill is hot, sear both sides of the steak over direct heat. Finish to your desired temperature with the lid closed. This is best medium-rare to medium (130 to 150°F). Let the steak rest at room temperature for about 10 to 15 minutes before slicing. Then, slice thin, against the grain of the meat.

12 BONES PASTRAMI BRINE

Yield: 3 quarts

2 quarts water
¾ cup kosher salt
½ cup dark brown sugar
2 tablespoons whole
　black peppercorns
2 tablespoons mustard seeds
2 tablespoons whole coriander

2 bay leaves
1 ounce fresh ginger, peeled and
　rough chopped (see page 66
　for a Pro tip on peeling ginger)
10 fresh garlic cloves, peeled
　and smashed
2 pounds ice

In a 4- to 6-quart pot, stir together all the ingredients except the ice. Simmer the mixture on low heat for approximately 30 minutes, stirring occasionally. Remove the brine from the heat, then cover and steep for another 30 minutes. Stir in the ice until it's melted. Transfer the cooled brine to a storage container with a lid and chill. The brine will be ready for use once it's fully cooled.

LIVERMUSH

As far as we know, livermush is a mostly a North Carolina obsession. At least we're the only ones who love it enough to throw more than one livermush festival a year. If you're making this recipe for the uninitiated, there's one thing you might want to keep in mind: Let them try it before you tell them what it is. They usually end up liking it more that way. Oh, and if they're from Pennsylvania, just tell them it's scrapple. (Livermush doesn't exactly sell anyone with its name.)

Traditionally, people like to serve livermush on toasted bread with slaw, mustard, and chili. At 12 Bones, we serve it with our Sweet Vinegar Coleslaw (page 126) and our Tangy Mustard Barbecue Sauce (page 115).

In a medium mixing bowl, mix together the ground pork, pork liver, tablespoon of salt, sage, black pepper, and pepper flakes with your hands, until the ingredients are fully incorporated. Cover the bowl and chill in the refrigerator.

Preheat the oven to 300°F. Grease an 8 x 4 x 4-inch bread pan, and then dust the bottom and the sides of the pan with the polenta. Set it aside.

Remove the meat mixture from the refrigerator, and heat a large skillet over medium-high heat. Brown the meat in the skillet, stirring occasionally to break it into small pieces. Once the meat is thoroughly cooked, remove it from the heat and set it aside.

In a medium saucepan, bring the stock and 1 teaspoon of salt to a boil. Reduce the heat to low, and then whisk in the polenta. Simmer the polenta, stirring frequently, until it just begins to thicken. This should take about 15 minutes. Remove the polenta from the heat and set it aside.

Yield: Up to 8 servings

- 2 pounds of ground pork (80/20 fat content)
- 4 ounces pork liver (fresh is better than frozen, and it should be dark brown rather than bluish or black, and moist but not slimy)
- 1 tablespoon kosher salt, plus 1 teaspoon
- 2 tablespoons fresh sage, minced
- 1 teaspoon ground black pepper
- ½ teaspoon red pepper flakes
- 1 cup 12 Bones Pork Stock (recipe follows, or use chicken stock)
- ¼ cup polenta, plus a bit extra for dusting the pan
  vegetable oil or bacon fat
- 1 large egg, lightly beaten

Once the meat is at room temperature, stir in the egg. Transfer half of the meat to a food processor and pulse until it becomes a paste-like consistency. Transfer that to a large mixing bowl, and then pulse the other half of the meat. Add that to the mixing bowl too. Stir in the polenta.

Press the meat and polenta mixture into the prepared bread pan, and cover it with foil. Put the loaf into the preheated oven and bake for 1 hour on the center rack of the oven. Once the time is up, remove the pan from the oven and uncover it. Cool the loaf to room temperature on a wire rack. Once cool, cover with plastic and chill for at least 2 hours or overnight.

To remove the loaf, place the bread pan directly on the stove top. Turn the heat up to medium for 1 minute. Remove the pan from the heat with oven mitts and place it on a heat-safe surface. Then, cut around the edges of the meat with a knife. Place a platter, upside down, over the top of the pan and quickly invert the pan and the platter. Tap on the bottom and the sides of the pan until the loaf releases. Remove the pan and slice the loaf, about a quarter-inch thick.

To finish the livermush, pour enough vegetable oil or bacon fat in the bottom of a large frying pan and heat over medium-high until the oil begins to shimmer. Fry livermush slices on each side until crispy on the outside. Do not overcrowd the slices.

12 BONES PORK STOCK

5 pounds smoked or roasted pork bones
2 yellow onions, quartered
1 carrot
1 celery stalk

1 tablespoon whole black peppercorns
1 bay leaf
2 gallons cold water

Add all ingredients to a large stockpot and bring to a boil. Reduce heat to low and simmer until reduced by half. Strain, reserving liquid, and discard bones and vegetables. Leftover stock can be frozen.

ingredient spotlight:
LIVERMUSH

Livermush was created by hog farmers who adhered to a whole-animal culture out of necessity. It's yet another example of subsistence cuisine turned tradition, a result of Southern families looking to find a way to use all the meaty bits that would come off a hog's head after boiling. "Waste not, want not," is a popular phrase in the South for a reason.

As anyone who has been around a barbecued whole hog knows, there are plenty of delectable morsels in a head, not the least of which are the cheeks. Mix those meaty bits with liver and cornmeal, and you have a nourishing but inexpensive meal made out of pieces that would otherwise go to waste.

Chef Shane was a toddler when he tried it for the first time, but he remembers that it was made from a fresh hog that his uncle had slaughtered. That's the other thing about livermush—if you were born and raised in North Carolina, it's likely that at least one of your relatives carries the family recipe on a yellowed index card.

Those of you from elsewhere need not turn up your noses, as this recipe has been adapted for people who don't have a hog in their backyard ready for slaughter.

Times are changing, and North Carolina is a swiftly growing state full of more and more transplants. That's particularly the case in Asheville, where mountain culture jockeys for space with city culture. But you can still buy livermush in the grocery stores. Even so, we believe the store-bought version doesn't hold a candle to our homemade version.

COCONUT MILK–BRAISED
BISON SHORT RIBS

This recipe came about when we had a local bison farmer stop by with some bison short ribs to try. We were impressed because, unlike beef short ribs, they aren't covered in fat.

The downside of that is that they can quickly become tough as nails. To work on improving that texture, and to bring out the rich flavor in these cuts, we experimented with marinades to help break down the meat. In this recipe, the acid in the coconut milk does the trick, helping to reduce the cooking time as well.

Note: You can substitute beef short ribs in this recipe. They are usually smaller, and tend to have a thick layer of fat on top and in the center of the rib. For best results, remove the top layer before marinating. Beef ribs also have a tendency to fall apart when cooking. We bind the meat tight to the rib with butcher's twine before braising.

Preheat the oven to 375°F. Line a baking pan with foil and spray it with nonstick spray.

Rinse the short ribs thoroughly under cold water to remove any bone fragments. This can be tedious; sometimes the bone fragments are forced into the meat and fat during the packing process. Next, drain the ribs and pat them dry. With a sharp knife, preferably a boning knife, remove the tough silverskin from the top of the ribs, exposing the meat.

Silverskin is connective tissue that can keep seasonings from penetrating the meat. It's also not excellent for eating. You may get ribs without this membrane, but if your ribs do have silverskin, removing it isn't a problem. Use a boning or paring knife to pull up a corner of the silverskin. You'll probably be able to pull it off the rest of the way with your fingers.

In a medium mixing bowl, whisk together the coconut milk and the tomato sauce. Using your hands, roll each rib portion in the mixture, one at a time, wiping the excess back into the bowl. Season each rib portion with 1 teaspoon of salt and then stand the ribs, meat-side up, on the prepared cookie sheet, without overcrowding them. This can be a little tricky, as the ribs would rather fall on their sides than stand at attention. Reserve the coconut-tomato mixture.

Yield: 6 servings

- 4 pounds bison short ribs, about 8 pieces
- 2 (14-ounce) cans of coconut milk
- 1 (29-ounce) can of tomato sauce
- 3 tablespoons kosher salt, plus 1 teaspoon
- 1 teaspoon ground cardamom (optional)
- ¼ cup 12 Bones Roasted Garlic (page 55) or, in a pinch, regular garlic, minced
- One Thai chili pepper, split (optional)
- 1 cup coconut water

Roast the ribs, uncovered in the oven, until the outside of the meat begins to caramelize. This should take 30 minutes, but check them after about 20. While the ribs are roasting, whisk the remaining ingredients—the 1 teaspoon of salt, the garlic, cardamom, chili pepper, and the reserved coconut water—into the coconut-tomato mixture to make a braising liquid. Pour half of the liquid into a 9 x 13-inch casserole dish or roasting pan.

Once the ribs are caramelized, remove them from the oven. Using a pair of tongs, stand ribs, meat-side up, in the braising liquid in the casserole dish, and then pour the remaining half of braising liquid over the top of the ribs. Wrap the pan with aluminum foil. Wrap tightly at the edges of the pan, but tent the foil in the middle so that it does not touch the meat.

Place the ribs in the oven, and then reduce the heat to 325°F. Bake until spoon-tender, which should take about 2 hours. Remove the ribs from the oven and, using tongs, transfer them to a large platter. Skim off the fat from the sauce with a large spoon, stir, and pour the skimmed sauce over the ribs.

SLOW-SMOKED PORK SHANKS

Just below the ham, but above the hock on a pig's hind legs, shanks are tough pieces of meat. They can be coaxed into tender juiciness, however, given enough time. Most shank recipes involve braising, but we searched for an alternative because we don't like ending up with almost as much fat as sauce in the braising pan.

We found shanks take perfectly to smoking. When you're cooking shanks on the smoker, most of the fat renders out. The fat that's left infuses the meat, keeping it moist but not too greasy. It's a win-win situation.

> **Note:** This recipe can be used for lamb shanks, which are easier to find. Still, we highly recommend the light flavor of pork shanks, so be sure to ask your butcher if he can find some for you. Serve them with mashed potatoes or grits and a nice, fresh salad.

Yield: 4 servings, 1 shank each

- 4 pork foreshanks (14–16 ounces)
- ⅓ cup kosher salt
- 4 teaspoons ground black pepper
- 1 cup 12 Bones Mop Sauce (page 105)
- 1 cup 12 Bones Chili-Ginger "Q" Sauce (page 66)

Preheat your smoker to 245 to 255°F, with only one side fired, or prepare a grill for indirect heat (see page 14 for full instructions). Soak a batch of apple or cherry wood chips for 30 minutes prior to cooking time, and then drain them before using. (See page 13 for more about smoking.)

Wash each shank to remove any bone fragments, then pat them dry with a clean towel. With a sharp knife, carefully cut the tendons all around the bottom—or small end—of the shank. Season the shanks with salt and pepper, then refrigerate them, uncovered, until the grill is ready. Once your smoker or grill is up to temperature, add the wood chips to the coals, or put them in a foil pouch on the hot side of the grill.

Smoke the shanks over the cool side with the grill or smoker lid closed, for about 1 hour. Mop the shanks and turn them. Adjust the coals or the chips to maintain the temperature and a heavy smoke during the process. Close the lid.

Repeat this process until the shanks are tender, about 4 hours total. Lift the lid and brush the shanks with the chili-ginger sauce, and then move to the hot side of the grill. Roll the shanks and brush them with the sauce until the entire shank has caramelized. Remove the shanks from the smoker and rest them at room temperature for 10 to 15 minutes before serving.

CHILI-GINGER "Q" SAUCE

This sauce is perfect for the pork shanks in the preceding recipe, but also works well for grilled chicken and chops.

Pro tip: Fresh ginger is a knobby, irregular thing. At first glance, it may seem hard to peel. Some use a paring knife or a peeler to remove the papery skin from this root, but this can create waste or worse: nicked fingers. But it's easy to peel using just a spoon, especially if the ginger is fresh (look for firm, smooth-skinned roots). Take a small spoon and, convex side down, scrape the edge of the utensil toward you, just as you would a peeler.

Heat oil in a 2-quart saucepan over low heat for two minutes, then sweat the ginger and the garlic on low heat in the oil until they have softened, taking care not to brown the garlic—doing so would make the sauce bitter. Add the cumin and the coriander, and stir until fragrant, which will take about 2 minutes. Stir in the ancho paste, and then add the soy sauce, citrus juice, and chili sauce, and bring to a boil over medium-high heat. Once the sauce comes to a boil, reduce heat to low, add Tomato "Q" sauce, and simmer until hot.

Yield: 2½ cups

- ¼ cup vegetable oil
- 1 ounce fresh ginger, peeled and minced
- 1 ounce garlic cloves, minced
- 1 teaspoon cumin
- 1 teaspoon coriander
- ¼ cup ancho paste (recipe follows, or look in the ethnic aisle of your local grocery store)
- ¼ cup soy sauce
- 3 tablespoons fresh lemon or lime juice
- 2 teaspoons Thai chili sauce
- 1½ cup 12 Bones Tomato "Q" Sauce (recipe on page 102)

ANCHO PASTE

1 pound dried ancho peppers
3 tablespoons vegetable oil
Water

Place the anchos in a stockpot large enough to hold the peppers and leave at least a 4-inch clearance. Cover the anchos with enough water to submerge. Bring the pot to a boil, and then remove it from the heat. Let it stand until the water is at room temperature. Strain. Remove the seeds and stems. Puree in a food processor until smooth. With the processor running, add just enough oil to keep the paste moving. Ancho paste can be frozen in an airtight container or an ice cube tray for future use.

CORNED BEEF BRISKET

Yield: 8 servings

- 1 4- to 5-pound flat brisket (the more marbling the better)
- 1 recipe Corned Beef Brine (page 68)
- 1 tablespoon mustard seed
- 1 bay leaf
- 1 tablespoon whole black peppercorns

Is corned beef really Irish? About as Irish as green beer, which is to say, not really. The Smithsonian, purveyor of well-researched history, says the Irish, by and large, couldn't afford beef until they immigrated to American big cities where they found the cheapish Jewish delis. According to the Smithsonian, Irish corned beef is actually Jewish corned beef brisket, a kosher cut from the front of the cow, thrown into a pot with cabbage and potatoes.

Still, 12 Bones' founder Sabra is Irish, and her husband came to love both cooking and eating this dish just for the tradition of it, even if it's a newer, Americanized tradition. But we love corned beef any day of the year and make it quite often. We try to stay away from things that are too traditional. To that end, we layer it on a sandwich with purple cabbage kraut and pepper jack, and smear it liberally with barbecue sauce spiked with mustard. That's our smokehouse twist on a Reuben, which we serve on Texas toast instead of rye.

Place the brisket in a 9 x 13-inch casserole dish. Stir the brine and pour it over the brisket. Cover and chill the brisket for at least three days, or up to six days, turning it every day. Remove the brisket from the brine and set it aside. Preheat oven to 325°F.

Strain the brine through a fine-meshed sieve into a 2- to 4-quart saucepan and then bring the brine to a boil over medium-high heat. Reduce the heat and simmer for an additional 10 minutes. Strain the hot brine through a fine-meshed sieve into a roasting pan. Add the mustard seeds, bay leaf, and peppercorns to the liquid and stir.

Carefully place the brisket in the roasting pan, and then cover the pan with foil. Bake the brisket in the center of the oven for 4 hours. Remove from the oven and uncover. Flip the brisket and then allow it to rest in the liquid for 15 minutes. Remove the brisket from the liquid and place it on a cutting board, allowing it to rest for an additional 15 minutes. Slice as thinly as possible, against the grain, and serve.

CORNED BEEF BRINE

Yield: 3 quarts, enough for one 4- to 5-pound brisket

2 quarts water
¾ cup kosher salt
½ cup dark brown sugar
2 cinnamon sticks
1 tablespoon whole cloves

1 tablespoon mustard seed
1 tablespoon whole allspice
2 bay leaves
1 tablespoon whole coriander
2 pounds ice

In a 4- to 6-quart pot, stir together all the ingredients except the ice. Simmer the mixture on low heat for approximately 30 minutes, stirring occasionally. Remove the brine from the heat, and then cover it and let it steep for another 30 minutes. Stir in the ice until it melts.

Transfer the cooled brine to a storage container with a lid and chill. The brine will be ready for use once fully cooled.

CORNED BEEF
SMOKED FATTY

The Smoked Fatty is our creative take on a bacon-wrapped meatloaf. The first one was an admittedly strange but delicious combination of pork, mozzarella cheese, and shitake mushrooms. The variations on this recipe are practically endless, and we definitely have a great time experimenting. Once you get the hang of this technique, you can also open it up to your own creative interpretation.

Make no mistake: This is a tricky recipe. Anything that involves making a bacon lattice is bound to be an expert-level dish. If you've ever made a lattice-crust pie, the method will make sense. If not, well, it may take you a few tries. But master it, and you'll be the master of the barbecue.

Place the grinder attachment parts of a stand-up mixer in the refrigerator and chill for 1 hour. Cover a 14 x 14-inch work surface with plastic wrap.

Lay out half of the bacon in the center of the plastic wrap horizontally, side by side, with each slice just barely touching the one right next to it. Starting at the top, fold every other piece back 1 inch. Lay a piece of the reserved bacon vertically on top of the unfolded pieces of bacon, and then lay the folded pieces of bacon back over the top of the newest piece. You have formed the first part of your lattice. Next, starting at the bottom, pull back the horizontal slices that you didn't fold over the first time, laying the next vertical piece of bacon down, just next to the first vertical piece. Repeat these steps until all of the bacon is used. Once the lattice is complete, it should resemble a woven meat rug. Lattices are, perhaps, easier to show than tell. See the visual guide on pages 70 to 71.

Assemble the grinder to the manufacturer's instructions, using the smallest die. Grind the meat directly into a large mixing bowl. Mix in the eggs and the Swiss cheese with gloved hands until well incorporated, and then place the meat mixture on your plastic-covered work surface. Form the meat into a 10-inch long, tight, even log in the

Yield: 10–12 portions
12 ounces bacon (about 16 slices)
3 pounds corned beef brisket, cut into cubes and chilled
2 large eggs, kept cold
8 ounces grated Swiss cheese

mixing bowl or on top of the lattice. Try to push out as much air as possible to prevent holes from forming inside your fatty while cooking.

Next, center your meat log 4 inches from the bottom of the lattice. Using the plastic wrap, lift the bottom of the lattice onto the log, and press gently to adhere the bacon to the ground meat. Carefully pull the plastic back and continue to roll and tighten, tucking bacon down on the ends of the fatty as you go. Once finished, the fatty should resemble a salami, wrapped in a bacon weave. Wrap tightly with the plastic wrap and chill for at least 30 minutes in the refrigerator.

Preheat the smoker or grill for indirect heat at 260 to 275°F. Soak a batch of apple or cherry wood chips in room temperature water for 30 minutes. (See page 13 for more about smoking.) Unwrap the fatty, and smoke with the lid closed until the internal temperature of the meat reaches 140°F. This should take about 30 minutes. Let the fatty rest at room temperature for about 30 minutes before slicing.

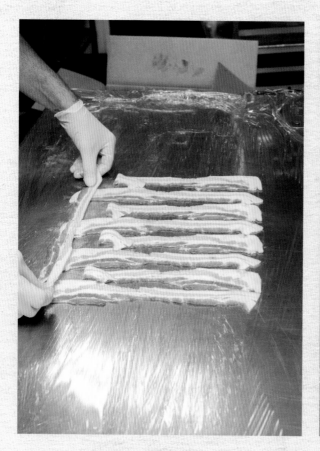 

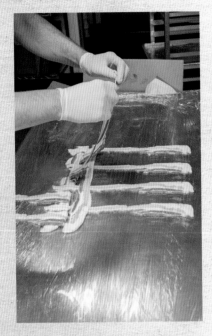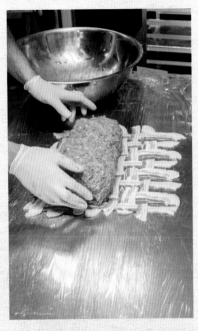

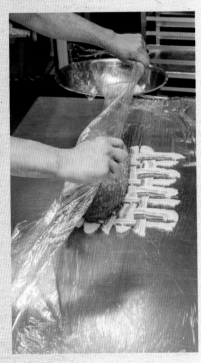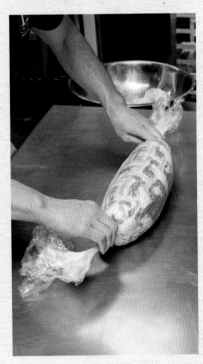

ROOT BEER OVEN-ROASTED BABY BACK RIBS

We get a lot of "root beer heads" at 12 Bones, and we created this recipe just for them. We also created this recipe for people who don't have the time or the equipment to smoke their ribs. This is one recipe that can be done mostly in the oven, though it calls for finishing on the grill so you can get that perfect crust.

You can use just about any soda you want to. It's the acid in the soda that helps tenderize the meat. Coca-Cola ribs? Sure. Cheerwine? No problem. Just don't leave out the fish sauce. It adds the perfect touch of salty *umami* to balance out that sweetness.

In a medium saucepan, bring the root beer, fish sauce, garlic, and pepper to a boil. Reduce the heat to low, then simmer until the liquid has been reduced by about half. Remove the reduction from the heat, and then stir in the water. Allow the sauce to rest until it cools to room temperature. Place the ribs in a roasting pan, pour the marinade over the ribs, cover, and then chill overnight or for at least 4 hours.

Preheat the oven to 325°F. Remove the ribs from the marinade, then transfer them to a baking sheet. Cover the ribs with foil, and bake for 2 hours, or until the meat is tender but not falling off the bone. Finish the ribs by grilling directly over high heat until the outside has caramelized, which should take about 4 minutes on each side.

Yield: 4–6 servings

- 4 cups of root beer
- ½ cup fish sauce
- 2 tablespoons minced garlic
- 1 tablespoon ground black pepper
- 2 cups cold water
- 2 racks baby back ribs

SMOKEHOUSE MEATLOAF

Yield: Serves a crowd. Big enough for five, or for a family, with enough leftovers for sandwiches.

3 pounds pork or beef, ground

2 eggs

1 poblano pepper, chopped

1 small onion, chopped

2 teaspoons, or more, (depending on taste) garlic, minced

2 teaspoons salt

1 cup Parmesan cheese, grated

This recipe calls for making what you might call a free-form loaf, which lets the hot air circulate, creating a nice crust around the whole exterior, rather than just the very top. Though some people think fat equals flavor, we think a solid brown crust is more important for a delicious meat dish. In fact, we make this meatloaf on a baking pan rather than in a loaf pan so that the fat runs out of the meat, instead of soaking into it. It's a little bit of a healthier method than most, but it still turns out to be perfectly moist.

This recipe yields a firm meatloaf, which lends itself well to rough handling without falling apart. We don't recommend you throw it about, but you can easily slice it into 1-inch-thick pieces well ahead of mealtime and then finish it over an extra-hot grill without it crumbling through the grates. Grilled is exactly how we serve this meatloaf at 12 Bones, and we find that the sear helps the flavor move to the next level. Serve with mashed potatoes, collard greens, and the barbecue sauce of your choice. (Sauces start on page 100.)

Preheat the oven to 325°F. Put the ground meat in a large mixing bowl. In a food processor, puree the egg, chopped poblano, onion, garlic, and salt. Add this mixture to the meat, then add the grated cheese. Mix together well, using your hands or a rubber spatula. Place the meat mixture on a greased baking pan, and shape it by hand into a loaf. Bake for 1 hour, or until the internal temperature is 165°F.

Note: At 12 Bones, we smoke our meatloaf with heavy smoke at 275°F for 1 hour and 30 minutes, or until the internal temperature is 150°F. Then, we cool the meatloaf, cut it into portions, and grill the slices over high, direct heat to finish.

beef and pork   73

BARBECUE
SCOTCH EGGS

Scotch eggs are meat-enrobed cooked eggs, breaded and then deep-fried. They have a history, but the problem is that no one quite knows which version to believe.

The London department store Fortnum & Mason swears up and down that it invented the Scotch egg in the era of horse-drawn carriage travel, for consumption on long trips. Others believe that the modern-day Scotch egg is a variant on a peasant-food dish, created especially for long days in the field. Others say it's a take on an Indian dish with many of the same components.

Whatever the case, there's plenty of protein in this tiny, deep-fried package, which would make for great fuel in a time when food was less plentiful. In this day of relative abundance, Scotch eggs have become a deep-fried pub snack to help soak up the pints. We've only served Barbecue Scotch Eggs at 12 Bones twice since they're so hard to make for the kind of volume that we serve here at the restaurant. But, as delicious as they are, we think they're worth the trouble for a smaller crowd.

Many choose to use a hard-boiled egg for this dish, which is certainly easier, but a soft-boiled egg, with its runny yolk, is much more satisfying. Being the type of restaurant that doesn't sacrifice quality for convenience, we chose the latter.

In a 4- to 6-quart saucepan, bring water to a boil over medium-high heat. Carefully add the eggs and remove from the heat immediately. Cover and steep for 7 minutes. Transfer the eggs to an ice bath for 1 minute. Carefully peel the eggs, starting with the fat end, under a drizzle of cold water. Set them aside.

Yield: 12 eggs

For the soft-boiled eggs:

3 quarts of water

12 large eggs, cold

For the Scotch eggs:

2 pounds smoked beef brisket cut in ½-inch cubes

1½ cup 12 Bones Tomato "Q" Sauce (page 102), or other sweet, tomato-based barbecue sauce

12 soft-boiled eggs, peeled

1 recipe 12 Bones Green Tomato Breading (below)

1½ quart frying oil

For the breading:

2 cups all-purpose flour

4 tablespoons 12 Bones Chicken Rub (page 26), divided

2 cups cornmeal

2 eggs

½ cup buttermilk

Note: It's not a bad idea to test out one egg before trying this recipe. People at higher or lower altitudes might find that the length of boiling time needs to be adjusted.

Pulse the brisket in food processor five times. Add the Tomato "Q" sauce, and puree the meat into a fine paste. Carefully encase the eggs with the chopped brisket to about ¼-inch thick, about 2½ ounces of meat per egg.

In a small mixing bowl, whisk together the flour and 2 tablespoons of Chicken Rub. Pour onto a dinner plate or a platter. In the same bowl, whisk together the cornmeal with the remaining Chicken Rub. Pour onto a separate plate or platter. In a separate bowl, whisk together the eggs and the buttermilk until smooth. Prepare a parchment-lined baking pan, and place within reach.

Dust the flour mixture onto a Scotch egg, then dip the Scotch egg in the buttermilk mixture until fully wet. Dredge the Scotch egg in the cornmeal mixture and shake off the excess. (Try to use one hand to handle the dry ingredients and the other hand to handle the wet ingredients.) Place egg on lined pan.

Repeat this process with the remaining eggs. If you end up needing more batter, you can make more.

Slowly and carefully preheat the oil in a 4-quart, heavy-bottomed saucepan to 375°F. Carefully drop the eggs into the heated oil, one at a time, in four batches in order to avoid overcrowding. (Allow the grease to come back to temperature between each batch.) Fry until golden brown. Remove with a slotted spoon and drain on a baking pan fitted with a wire rack or paper towels. Serve hot.

III poultry and seafood

Man cannot survive on pork alone. Or so we've heard. Still we find plenty of room on our menu for the folks who don't do beef or pork, or simply want a break from it.

Poultry has plenty to recommend it anyway. What's better than the crispy exterior of a chicken thigh, laced with smoke and perfectly bronzed? In fact, many of our regulars swear by the chicken. One of them, Guy Picard, eats at 12 Bones several times a week with his wife Judy. He frequently orders the half-smoked chicken and maintains that it not only tastes good but keeps him in shape. "I eat at 12 Bones Tuesday through Saturday," says Guy. "I maintain my weight by eating there daily."

If you're not craving smoked chicken after that kind of testimonial, go ahead and skip this chapter. But if you'd like to know how to make your own delicious chicken, as well as some of the best wings, shrimp cakes, and Thanksgiving turkeys you'll ever eat, read on.

WHOLE-SMOKED CHICKEN

Smoked chicken is actually Chef Shane's favorite thing on the menu because it's smoky but still moist and crispy on the outside. And it's a great alternative to fattier pork. Hey, sometimes even chefs have to watch their waistlines. We think you'll love it just as much, but more for the fact that it's delicious.

Yield: About 4 servings

- 1   3- to 3½-pound whole chicken
- 2   tablespoons 12 Bones Chicken Rub (page 26)

Season your chicken with the rub, being sure to work the seasoning thoroughly over the entire surface. Chill the rubbed-down bird for 1 hour in the refrigerator. Meanwhile, soak the wood chips in room-temperature water for about 30 minutes. Prepare the smoker or grill for smoking at a temperature between 260 and 275°F by pushing the charcoal briquettes to one side of the smoker or grill, or by turning on one side of a gas grill. (See page 13 for more instructions on smoking.)

Drain the water from the wood chips. Once the flames are out and the coals are hot and covered in white ash, add wood chips, or make a smoking packet for a gas grill as described on page 14. Place the chicken on the grill, on the opposite side from the heat, then close the lid of the grill. Smoke the chicken at a temperature of 260 to 275°F, or until the internal temperature of the meat at the thickest part of the thigh reaches 165°F, according to your meat thermometer.

Remove the chicken from the grill and then let it rest for about 30 minutes at room temperature. Add fresh coals to the grill in an even layer, or turn up the heat on the gas grill to medium-high. Once the grill reaches a temperature between 375 and 400°F, cut the chicken in half, and put it back on the grill, skin-side down, letting it brown until the skin is perfectly crispy. Serve hot, or let cool and pull the meat for chicken salads.

SMOKY CHICKEN WINGS

We aren't exactly a wing place, but people still love our take on wings. The secret is the cooking process, a multistep method. The wings are first smoked, cooled off, and then fried, so they get nice and crispy on the outside. Even after all that frying, they're permeated with a deep smokehouse flavor our customers have come to expect from us. That multistep process also means that these wings are great for tailgating, since you can smoke them ahead of time and fry them when it's time to serve. (It's OK to finish them on the grill, too, just as long as you get the grill hot enough to sear a thick crust on the surface of the wing).

Dry off the wings with a paper towel, and then toss them with brown sugar and salt. Prepare a grill or smoker for indirect heat at 275°F by pushing lit coals to one side or only turning on one side of your gas grill (see page 13 for a more thorough smoking explanation). Soak some light-flavored wood chips in room-temperature water for at least 30 minutes (wood details on page 18). Smoke the wings for 30 minutes, cool them on a drying rack and refrigerate until ready to fry and serve. Or, if you're ready to eat, go ahead and preheat the frying oil in a heavy-bottomed saucepan until it reaches 375°F. Carefully fry wings in the oil until they are crispy, drain on a paper towel, and then serve, tossed in your choice of sauce (or keep it on the side).

Though you can use any variety of sauce to coat these wings, our Spicy Thai Chicken Wing Sauce (recipe at right) is a big hit at the restaurant.

Yield: 8–10 servings

- 5 pounds jumbo chicken wings
- ¾ cup dark brown sugar
- 1½ tablespoons kosher salt
- 1½ quarts frying oil
- Spicy Thai Chicken Wing Sauce (optional)

SPICY THAI CHICKEN WING SAUCE

We use this for wing sauce, but it can also be used to baste baked chicken.

3 tablespoons peanut oil
1 shallot, minced
5 cloves garlic, minced
1 tablespoon fresh ginger, peeled
    and minced
½ cup coconut milk
1 cup creamy peanut butter
1 teaspoon dark brown sugar

1 can coconut water (11.8 ounces)
2 limes, zest and juice
    (preferably unwaxed)
1 tablespoon Sriracha hot sauce
1 tablespoon soy sauce
3 tablespoons cilantro,
    chopped (optional)

Heat the oil in a small saucepan over medium heat for 30 seconds. Next, add
the shallot, garlic, and ginger, and then stir the sauce constantly for 3 minutes.
Remove from the heat, then stir in the coconut milk, peanut butter, and dark
brown sugar. Transfer the sauce to a blender or food processor. Add the
coconut water, the lime zest and juice, the Sriracha, soy sauce, and cilantro, and
pulse until smooth.

SMOKED SHRIMP

This recipe creates the star of the show for a bowl of shrimp and grits, a classic Low-Country dish, or Smoked Shrimp Cakes (page 85). These smoky shrimp are also a welcome addition in a summer salad, with plenty of roasted corn kernels, chopped tomatoes, and basil. Or just serve them on a plate and watch them disappear.

The sour cream used in this recipe helps keep the shrimp moist and absorbs the flavor of the smoke, but doesn't affect the flavor of the final dish.

Prepare a grill or smoker for indirect heat at 275°F by pushing lit coals to one side or only turning on one side of your gas grill (see page 13 for a more thorough smoking explanation). Soak some light-flavored wood chips in room-temperature water for at least 30 minutes (wood details on page 18). In a small mixing bowl, whisk together the sour cream and the chicken rub. Toss the shrimp in the sour cream mixture, then place the shrimp on a wire rack set into a baking pan large enough to accommodate it. Smoke for 10 to 12 minutes. Serve immediately, or use in the following recipes.

Yield: 1 serving, because they're so darn good.

- 1 pound large shrimp (21-30), shell on (reserve shells for smoky spiced shrimp sauce)
- 2 tablespoons sour cream
- 2 tablespoons 12 Bones Chicken Rub (page 26)

SMOKY SPICED SHRIMP AND GRITS

This is our smokified take on the Low-Country classic, shrimp and grits. The smoky shrimp are an excellent pairing with the creamy, spicy grits (page 173), and the spiced shrimp sauce in the following recipe really takes it over the top. This is a filling mess of food that's perfect as a one-dish meal. No sides required.

Yield: 4 servings

- 2 tablespoons butter
- Smoked shrimp shells from Smoked Shrimp recipe
- 1 large shallot, minced
- 5 cloves 12 Bones Roasted Garlic (page 55), smashed
- 1 (15-ounce) can crushed tomatoes
- 1 cup heavy cream
- 1 teaspoon hot sauce, such as Sriracha

- 1 teaspoon dark brown sugar
- 1 teaspoon ground cumin
- ¼ teaspoon ground cloves
- ¼ teaspoon ground cinnamon
- ¼ teaspoon ground nutmeg
- 1 teaspoon kosher salt
- ¼ teaspoon ground black pepper
- 2 tablespoons finely chopped cilantro (optional)

Melt the butter in a 2- to 3-quart saucepan or large sauté pan over medium heat. Once the butter has melted and begins to bubble (but not brown), add the shrimp shells, the shallot, and the garlic. Stir constantly, until the garlic and shallots are golden. Add the crushed tomatoes and loosen any sticky stuff that remains in the bottom of the pan using a wooden spoon. Once the pan is deglazed, stir in the remaining ingredients, except for the cilantro, and reduce the heat to low.

Simmer for 30 minutes, stirring every few minutes to prevent scorching, then taste and adjust seasonings as necessary. Strain the sauce through a fine-mesh strainer, directly onto the Smoked Shrimp and Jalapeño Cheese Grits, and then garnish with cilantro.

SMOKED SHRIMP CAKES

**Yield: 6 cakes,
one per serving**

- 1 recipe 12 Bones Smoked Shrimp (page 82)
- 2 eggs, lightly beaten
- 1 tablespoon Dijon mustard
- 1 tablespoon Worcestershire sauce
- ½ teaspoon Sriracha sauce
- 1 cup finely crushed saltine crackers
- ½ cup mayonnaise
- 1 teaspoon kosher salt
- ½ cup vegetable oil

This is a delicious way to turn smoked shrimp into a deceptively simple summer meal. Fashioned into smaller patties, these cakes make perfect appetizers for a crowd, or they can be built into a main dish for up to six people. For easy mains, serve the cakes with tartar sauce, a wedge of lemon, and a lightly dressed leaf-lettuce salad. Or serve them on toasted English muffins with a smear of mayo and crisp lettuce leaves.

Prepare the shrimp according to the recipe on page 82. Shell the shrimp and chop the meat finely. Set the shells aside to make the Smoky Spiced Shrimp Sauce (page 82), which can be used on these cakes or with the Smoked Shrimp and Jalapeño Cheese Grits.

In a large bowl, gently mix all the ingredients until they are well combined. Shape into six, 1-inch-thick cakes, and transfer the cakes to a waxed paper–lined plate. Refrigerate for 30 minutes, uncovered. Meanwhile, preheat the oven to 400°F.

Heat the vegetable oil in a large, cast-iron skillet or sauté pan over medium heat for 2 minutes. Carefully add the shrimp cakes and then cook until the bottoms are golden-brown and crisp. Using a slotted metal spatula, carefully turn the cakes over and transfer the whole pan carefully into the preheated oven. Bake for 10 minutes, or until the edges are pleasantly crisp and the cake is firm. Remove from the oven and then drain on a plate lined with paper towels.

SMOKED
WHOLE TURKEY

The day before Thanksgiving, 12 Bones is open for business. We serve our regular large lunch crowd, but we're also busy filling orders for the big turkey day dinner table. We see the same faces year after year coming to pick up their Thanksgiving dinner, which includes this smoked turkey as well as the cranberry barbecue sauce on page 92 and the gravy on page 95.

This recipe calls for giving the turkey a long soak in the brine (recipe for Turkey Brine follows), but large turkeys require large pots in which to keep them. If you have a hard time finding a container that's large enough to fit into your fridge, you can use a large turkey-basting bag. Just be sure to seal the bag tightly. It wouldn't be a bad idea to double bag. Set the whole thing in a roasting pan and then put it in the refrigerator. Always refrigerate. No exceptions.

Remove the neck and giblets from the turkey, and set them aside in the refrigerator for use in turkey gravy (page 95). Place the turkey in a container large enough to leave 2 inches of space on all sides and over the top of the bird. Stir the chilled brine and then pour it over the turkey. Cover and chill for 8 to 12 hours, but no longer than 12, or the bird will be too salty.

Yield: 8 servings
1 12–14 pound turkey, thawed
1 recipe 12 Bones Turkey Brine (follows)
3 tablespoons 12 Bones Turkey Rub (follows, or substitute 12 Bones Chicken Rub, page 26)

TURKEY BRINE

1 gallon of water
1 cup of 12 Bones
   Chicken Rub (page 26) or
   Turkey Rub (page 87)
½ cup salt

Heat over medium heat until salt and spices are dissolved without boiling. Stir the ingredients with a whisk and then chill until ready to use.

Prepare a grill or smoker for indirect heat at 275°F by pushing lit coals to one side or only turning on one side of your gas grill (see page 13 for a more thorough smoking explanation), and soak some apple wood, or other lighter wood, chips or chunks in room-temperature water for at least 30 minutes. Remove the turkey from the brine, draining off as much liquid as possible, paying close attention to the bird's cavity. Then pat it dry with a clean towel. Dust the outside of the turkey with the turkey rub.

Smoke the turkey over indirect heat, breast up, with the smoker lid closed, until the internal temperature of the bird reaches 165°F at the thickest part of the breast, and the skin is golden brown. This should take 20 to 25 minutes per pound. Remove the bird from the smoker and allow it to rest for 30 minutes at room temperature before carving.

TURKEY RUB

We use this rub on our smoked turkeys, but it's also an excellent seasoning for a standard, oven-roasted Thanksgiving turkey. The only caution we have is that cooking this rub at a temperature higher than 300°F will change the flavor of the herbs and sugar. In general, we only use it for low-temperature smoking. We felt this rub needed an herb to set it apart from the others, so thyme, a favorite of ours, became the prominent flavor.

<u>Yield: 2 cups</u>

- 5 tablespoons iodized salt
- 6 tablespoons paprika
- 6 tablespoons granulated garlic
- 5 tablespoons dark brown sugar
- 3 tablespoons dried thyme
- 2 tablespoons coarse-ground black pepper
- 3 tablespoons granulated onion
- 3 tablespoons dried basil
- 1½ teaspoons cayenne

Combine all the ingredients thoroughly, leaving no lumps. Store in an airtight container.

SMOKED TURKEY BREAST

We go through a lot of smoked turkey breast—much of it goes out of the kitchen paired with Brie and our Brown Sugar Bacon on our most popular sandwich (page 90).

The thing about this recipe, though, is that it's quite versatile. Juicy turkey is equally at home on the dinner table, in a quesadilla, or as the basis for a smoky stew, especially if you're looking for an alternative to bacon that imparts a lot of flavor with only a fraction of the fat. For that matter, this turkey is also excellent chopped and scattered over lettuce leaves with a few sliced hard-boiled eggs.

Yield: 4–6 servings, depending on the size of the breast

1 boneless, skin-on turkey breast (these will average about 2 pounds)

Approximately 2 tablespoons 12 Bones Turkey Rub (page 87) or poultry seasoning

But before you go imagining turkey breast added to all your favorite dishes, you'll have to master the technique. The trick to keeping this turkey moist is to smoke this bird just up to temp, but without overcooking it. Sounds easy enough right? But it may take a time or two and close attention toward the end to get it right. After that, it's all about how you slice it, and keeping this turkey nice and thin is the way to go.

Remove the skin from the turkey breast, reserving it for later use. Coat the surface of the breast with rub. Place the turkey, uncovered, in the refrigerator. Prepare a grill or smoker for indirect heat at 275°F by pushing lit coals to one side or only turning on one side of your gas grill (see page 13 for a more thorough smoking explanation), and soak some applewood, or other lighter wood, chips in room-temperature water for at least 30 minutes. Layer the smoker rack with the turkey skin to catch the moisture from the breast. Lay the breast on top of the skin and smoke with the lid closed until internal temperature reaches about 140°F, which will take approximately 40 to 50 minutes.

Remove the turkey breast from the smoker and rest, uncovered, at room temperature for about 20 minutes before carving.

Note: If you're using wood chips, oak is the best choice for this dish.

THE 12 BONES TURKEY SANDWICH

Who goes to a smokehouse and eats a turkey sandwich? Hundreds of people weekly, that's who. This killer dish gets thinly sliced Smoked Turkey Breast, plus Brie, 12 Bones Brown Sugar Bacon and Sun-dried Tomato Pesto Mayo, all on Texas toast. You just learned the secrets for the turkey, so here are the rest of the components:

5 ounces of 12 Bones Smoked Turkey Breast, thinly sliced

2 slices of Texas toast

Generous smear of Sun-dried Tomato Pesto Mayo (recipe follows)

2 slices of Brie cheese

2 pieces of 12 Bones Sugar Bacon (page 41)

Heat up the turkey. Meanwhile, toast the bread. Add pesto mayo to the inside of each slice of bread. Add the turkey to one piece, then the Brie, and then layer the bacon on top. Close up your sandwich, and then enjoy a 12 Bones favorite.

SUN-DRIED TOMATO PESTO MAYO

Whatever pesto you don't use can be folded into pasta or used as a dip for veggies. You can even use it in an omelet. This yields 2 cups of pesto, which will make 4 cups of pesto mayo. Simply fold one part pesto into one part mayo.

FOR THE PESTO:

4   ounces fresh basil (about 2 cups)

⅓ cup sun-dried tomatoes

¾ cup vegetable oil, divided

2   tablespoons sunflower seeds

3   cloves garlic

1   teaspoon kosher salt

½ cup grated Parmesan cheese

Remove the basil leaves from the stems and then rough chop them. Set aside. Then add the sun-dried tomatoes to a food processor. Turn on the food processor and, while it is running, slowly drizzle in 3 tablespoons of oil. Stop the food processor and add sunflower seeds, garlic, salt, and basil leaves. Turn the processor back on and, while it is running, drizzle in the remaining oil. Turn off the processor as soon as the oil is incorporated. Transfer the finished pesto to a mixing bowl and fold in the grated Parmesan. Taste and adjust seasoning as needed. Place leftover pesto in nonreactive container and lay plastic wrap directly on top of pesto, being sure to squeeze out any air bubbles. Cover container and chill up to seven days. Pesto can also be frozen in a freezer bag. Be sure to squeeze out as much air as possible before sealing bag to prevent freezer burn and discoloration. Thaw completely and stir before serving.

CRANBERRY
BARBECUE SAUCE

Cranberry sauce does not exactly take a prominent place in the lore of barbecue, but we aren't the most traditional of folks. And, as Chef Shane says, "We had to put something on the menu for the Yankees." A Yankee berry this is; in the United States, cranberries are most often cultivated in the North, particularly in Massachusetts, New Jersey, and Wisconsin. They're harvested, generally, between Labor Day and Christmas, which is why they've become so closely associated with the holiday season.

To that end, this is a fun sauce to serve with a nontraditional Thanksgiving turkey dinner (we sell a lot of it with smoked turkey in November), but it's also great on pork, especially once fall arrives. It's a sweet sauce when it first hits the palate, but the tanginess from the cranberries lingers on the tongue. The poblano gives it just a hint of heat, but you may leave it out entirely if you want. Or, since the heat comes from the seeds and ribs of the pepper, remove those for a milder sauce.

Heat the vegetable oil in a medium saucepan over medium-low heat for 1 minute. Stir in the diced yellow onion, and the red, green, and poblano peppers, and cook until the vegetables soften, stirring and taking care not to brown the onions. This should take about 5 minutes.

Remove the pan from the heat, and then transfer the veggies into a food processor or blender. Puree the veggies with the cranberries and cranberry juice until the mixture is smooth. Then return it to the saucepan, add the remaining ingredients, and simmer over low heat for 30 minutes, stirring occasionally. Remove from the heat.

Once cooled, this sauce can be stored in an airtight container and chilled for up to one week.

Yield: About 4 cups, or eight ½-cup servings

- 2 tablespoons of vegetable oil
- ¼ cup diced yellow onion
- 2 tablespoons diced red bell pepper
- 2 tablespoons diced green bell pepper
- 1 tablespoon diced poblano pepper (optional)
- 12 ounces fresh cranberries
- ⅔ cup cranberry juice, unsweetened
- ⅔ cup cider vinegar
- 1 tablespoon jerk seasoning (store bought, or make the recipe on page 53)
- ⅓ cup sugar
- 1⅓ cup of 12 Bones Tomato "Q" Sauce (page 102)

SMOKY
TURKEY GRAVY

Yield: 3–4 cups

Neck, heart, liver, and gizzards from 1 turkey

4 tablespoons butter

1 small onion, chopped

5 cloves of garlic, rough chopped

½ cup flour

3 cups 12 Bones Pork Stock (recipe on page 59, or use store-bought chicken stock)

1 cup whole milk

1 teaspoon 12 Bones Chicken Rub (page 26) or poultry seasoning

½ teaspoon vanilla extract

4 teaspoons Worcestershire sauce

1 teaspoon kosher salt

1 teaspoon coarse-ground black pepper

½ teaspoon ground cumin

½ teaspoon paprika

½ teaspoon dry English mustard

This is not a gravy for beginners. If you have the means to smoke the necks and gizzards for this recipe, it's definitely preferred, but we've added an alternative for those who aren't the smoking type. We really like the way the smoke plays off the offal, but it's your prerogative. And it practically goes without saying that this gravy won't be smoky if it's done in the oven, right?

This is great over roasted turkey, of course, but it also makes a perfect leftover turkey sandwich spread. Also, don't be afraid to pour this liberally over biscuits.

Prepare a grill or smoker for indirect heat at 260 to 275°F by pushing lit coals to one side or only turning on one side of your gas grill (see page 13 for a more thorough smoking explanation), and soak wood chips of your choice in room-temperature water for at least 30 minutes. If you don't have access to a smoker, roast the turkey parts, with a touch of oil, in an oven-safe sauté pan at 400°F for 15 to 20 minutes or until dark brown.

Melt the butter in a heavy-bottomed, 4-quart saucepan. Add the onion and garlic, and sweat on low heat, just until the onions are translucent. Add the flour all at once, and continue to stir every 30 seconds or so, until the roux turns medium-brown in color. While whisking, add all the remaining ingredients whisking and simmer on low heat.

Just as the gravy starts to thicken, remove and discard the neck. Remove from heat, and then puree the gravy in a blender or a food processor. Strain the gravy into a pan through a fine-mesh sieve, using a wooden spoon to help force the gravy through. To finish, simmer the gravy on low heat to the desired thickness, and adjust the seasoning to taste.

CHICKEN KIMCHI
MEATBALLS

Angela's Korean mother comes to visit us from time to time and, like any mother will tend to do, cooks as though she is feeding an army. Once she made so much kimchi, it wouldn't fit in the fridge. We happened to have some boneless chicken thighs on hand and some extra cilantro, so we ground up the chicken, added the kimchi and herbs, and added about every Asian spice we had until something worked. We were shocked by how delicious it tasted, and it's a special we still trot out from time to time. There's more about Mrs. Koh on page 161, as well as a couple of kimchi recipes.

Preheat the oven to 400°F. In a large mixing bowl, thoroughly combine all the ingredients, except for the Bacon Sugar. Roll the chicken mixture into slightly smaller than golf ball-size balls, and roll each ball in the Bacon Sugar. Place the meatballs, just lightly touching, on a parchment-lined baking sheet. Bake for 15 minutes, or until lightly browned and cooked through. Allow to rest at room temperature for 10 minutes before serving.

Pro tip: 12 Bones Jalapeño "Q" Sauce makes these balls sing.

Yield: 10–12 balls

- 1 pound ground chicken thighs
- 3 tablespoons fish sauce
- 1 large shallot, minced
- 1 teaspoon garlic, minced
- 3 tablespoons chopped cilantro
- 1 tablespoon cornstarch
- ½ teaspoon kosher salt
- 1 cup kimchi, drained and chopped (store-bought or use the recipe on page 162)
- ½ cup 12 Bones Bacon Sugar (page 41)

SMOKED CHICKEN SHEPHERD'S PIE

Shepherd's pie is a hearty, classic dish, and perhaps the best use of leftovers in the history of leftovers. Though it has a Southern comfort-food reputation, Shepherd's pie comes from an old European tradition of meat pies. According to the *Oxford Companion to Food*, the dish likely originated in northern England and Scotland and was made with shepherd's mutton, hence the name.

This version doesn't contain mutton, though you could certainly substitute any cooked meat you'd like for the smoked chicken, particularly come Thanksgiving, when the leftover mashed potatoes and turkey are plentiful.

At 12 Bones, we offer our smoked chicken in halves and quarters, and some days we'll only sell out of the white meat. This recipe helps us figure out what to do with the rest of the bird at the end of the day. The smoked chicken gives the Shepherd's pie a rich, smokehouse flavor. For a lower-fat recipe, you can leave the bacon out. Just sauté the onion, celery, and carrot in a tablespoon of olive oil, instead.

In a large skillet, cook the bacon over medium heat until it begins to crisp. Add the onion, celery, and carrot, and stir for 2 minutes. Add the stock, and then raise the heat to medium-high. Reduce the liquid by half. Stir in the chicken, cilantro, and sage, then remove the mixture from the heat and season it with salt and pepper. Pour the filling into a 9 x 12-inch casserole dish, and then cool the filling to room temperature. Preheat the oven to 400°F.

Yield: 4–6 servings
4 ounces (about 4–5 slices) bacon, chopped
1 medium onion, chopped
1 medium celery rib, chopped
1 medium carrot, chopped
2 cups chicken stock
1 smoked chicken, pulled from the bone and chopped
1 tablespoon fresh cilantro, chopped (you may substitute parsley)
1 tablespoon fresh sage, chopped
3 cups mashed potatoes
2 tablespoons minced chives
Salt and pepper to taste
1 large egg, beaten
2 cups sharp cheddar cheese, grated

In a large bowl, mix together the potatoes and the chives. Taste the mixture and, if needed, season it with salt and pepper to taste. Then, stir the egg into the potatoes. Once it's fully incorporated, spread the potato mixture over the top of the filling, then sprinkle with cheddar cheese. Bake, uncovered, for 30 minutes, or until the top is browned and the filling is bubbling. Remove it from the oven, and allow it to stand at room temperature for 10 minutes before serving.

the Mikes' take on:
SPECIALS

Mike Moore and Mike Thakar came to Asheville from California, by way of New York City. Moore and Thaker have traveled the world, biked through Tuscany, dined in Hong Kong and witnessed firsthand the new-American food revolution, ushered through California by Alice Waters of Chez Panisse and Thomas Keller of the French Laundry. And they now count among their favorite sensory experiences their weekly pilgrimages to 12 Bones.

"We were in the Bay Area in the prime Alice Waters era," says Moore. "The best tricks we learned from the people who worked in those restaurants was finding out where they ate. Where does the waiter from Chez Panisse eat on his day off?"

12 Bones, says Moore, is the sort of place where restaurant professionals eat on their days off in Asheville. Not too fussy, yet with enough elegance and variety to the menu for wide appeal—and to make frequent visits interesting. "They push the edges of what they do without getting into things they can't do well," Moore noted. "I've never had anything I didn't think was delicious."

In the five years that they've lived in the Asheville area, the couple makes at least two weekly trips to 12 Bones to fill up on lunch. "Typically, we eat and then go to the takeout counter and get ribs and/or a roasted chicken, and we get enough for a dinner for at least two, more if we're entertaining," says Moore. "It's like a Saturday routine for us when we're running errands."

Still, he added, 12 Bones really shines when it comes to special, off-the-menu items, many of which can be found in this book.

"We often run out there just for the special that day," Moore says, noting the "killer" Reuben, and the "amazing" Cuban sandwich in particular. He also waxes poetic about the mushroom and sausage casserole on page 179 and the "very, very good" meatloaf on page 73, a version he says hits the spot when he's in "classic comfort-food mode." And here you thought all meatloaf was created equal.

IV big, bad barbecue sauces

At 12 Bones, we're not the type of restaurant that sticks stubbornly to North Carolina barbecue. We showcase the best of the South, including tastes of Tennessee and South Carolina. We love our sweet tomato sauces, just like they do in Kansas City. We honor South Carolina with our Tangy Mustard Barbecue Sauce. And the Jalapeño "Q" Sauce reaches the level of heat Texans seem to love.

We also cherry-pick a few flavors from regions outside of the South too. (Our founding owner, Sabra, is a Yankee through and through, which you'll taste in recipes like the Cranberry-Jalapeño "Q" Sauce.) Some flavors are completely unique to us as well, such as our famous Blueberry-Chipotle Sauce, which owes its flavor only to our imaginations.

We'll provide a few pairing suggestions here and there, but feel free to use the following sauces as you see fit.

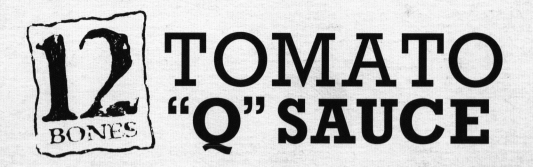

TOMATO "Q" SAUCE

This recipe is a workhorse in our kitchens. We use this to build other sauces and include it in several recipes, including our Smoky Baked Beans. We love to serve it with our "Nekkid" Ribs as well (page 28). Consider it somewhat of a mother sauce, 12 Bones style.

This sauce will taste its best within a few weeks if refrigerated, or you can portion it out into smaller plastic containers and freeze it. Even better, if you know how to can, this stuff will keep practically forever.

Let Tom Q, as we call it in the restaurant, be a workhorse for you too. Smear it on burgers, chicken—you name it. Do note that this is a very mild, somewhat sweet sauce. If you'd like to try on a spicier sauce for size, check out the Pineapple-Habanero Barbecue Sauce on page 120. It's a variation of this sauce that will put a little hair on your chest.

Combine all ingredients in a medium-size saucepan and simmer on low heat until all the dry ingredients have dissolved, stirring occasionally with a whisk. Note that mustard powder can be a bit hard to dissolve.

Yield: 4 cups

- 3 cups ketchup
- ⅔ cup cider vinegar
- ½ cup blackstrap molasses
- 6 tablespoons Worcestershire sauce
- 6 tablespoons dark brown sugar
- 1 teaspoon granulated garlic
- 1 teaspoon granulated onion
- 1 teaspoon dry English mustard
- 1 teaspoon black pepper
- 1 teaspoon salt

Sweet Tomato
BARBECUE SAUCE

12
BONES
smokehouse

12 oz

MADE WITH LOVE IN ASHEVILLE, NC

ingredient spotlight:

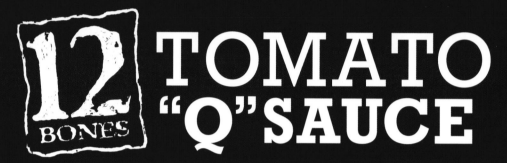

TOMATO "Q" SAUCE

Who knew the Democratic National Convention (DNC) needed its own barbecue sauce? Apparently, it required three.

First held in 1832, one of the DNC's chief goals, among other things (like nominating potential presidents), is to unify the party. But it would take something more like an act of God to bring together the various factions of the barbecue world, even those within the Carolinas. Thus, it made sense that the 2012 DNC, which was held in Charlotte, North Carolina, selected three very different official barbecue sauces to appease three very different regions. There was a mustard-based sauce for South Carolina, a vinegar-based sauce for eastern North Carolina, and a sweet, tomato-based sauce for Western North Carolina. Out of 20 tomato-based sauces, 12 Bones beat the competition.

Now, you can find our winning sauce in bottles in select grocery stores, labeled "12 Bones Sweet Tomato Barbecue Sauce." Yep, it's a mouthful. That's why we call it "Tom Q" in the restaurant.

What can you make with 12 Bones Tomato "Q" Sauce? Quite a lot, actually. It's a key factor in many of our recipes, including the following five sauces and spreads.

MOP SAUCE

What, pray tell, is Mop Sauce? It's a flavorful moistening agent that you'll find in many of our slow-cooking recipes. It's for keeping the meat juicy while it's smoking, and for giving it just a hint of flavor to boot. A mix of stock and Tomato "Q" Sauce, this Mop Sauce adds a lot of flavor without running off the meat, but it doesn't mask other flavors and spices we use in our recipes.

Why dilute the Tomato "Q" at all? With experience, we found that regular barbecue sauce is too thick and eventually burns in most slow-cooking recipes—no matter how talented the chef.

As far as recipes go, this one's about as simple as it gets: Whisk together equal parts 12 Bones Tomato "Q" with 12 Bones Pork Stock (page 59) or any store-bought chicken stock.

JAMAICAN JERK
BARBECUE SAUCE

While making this recipe, watch your eyes and wash your hands—this sauce bites back. It gets its heat from habaneros, as is traditional with the tapestry of flavors that jerk sauce typically requires. Though this sauce is our own take on traditions, you'll find the flavors adhere fairly closely to what you might find in the islands.

Jerk sauce is perfect with slow-smoked chicken, though Jamaicans are known to slather theirs on beef, fish, and even goat. We think you'll find it perfectly versatile. Not a fan of heat? Leave the peppers out of the recipe.

In a small saucepan, stir together the juice and the jerk seasoning. Add the habanero peppers, stir, and then simmer until the mixture is reduced by half. Carefully puree the sauce in a food processor or blender with the Tomato "Q" sauce until the mixture is smooth.

Yield: 2½ cups

- 3 cups pineapple juice
- ¼ cup jerk seasoning (see page 53 or purchase some in your local grocery store)
- 3 dried habaneros
- 1 cup 12 Bones Tomato "Q" Sauce (page 102)

ANCHO-GINGER
BARBECUE SAUCE

Yield: 2 cups

- ½ cup ancho paste (see page 66, or look in the ethnic food aisle)
- ¼ cup brown sugar
- ¼ cup water
- ½ ounce fresh ginger, peeled and rough chopped
- 3 cloves fresh garlic
- 1 cup 12 Bones Tomato "Q" Sauce (page 102)

This barbecue sauce is great with grilled seafood. The ancho gives it a mild heat, but it's not an overpowering, wash-your-mouth-out kind of heat. The flavor of the ginger lingers, and the sugar acts as a balancing agent. This sauce plays well with a versatile array of meats, but we'd advise you to stick to the lighter meats, such as chicken and pork.

Try this with the Oven-Roasted Pulled Pork Butt on page 37.

Place all the ingredients, except for the Tomato "Q" sauce, in a food processor or blender, and blend until smooth. Transfer the ingredients to a saucepan and simmer on low for 15 to 20 minutes.

BBQ
THOUSAND ISLAND

Yield: ¾ cup

- ½ cup mayonnaise
- 1 tablespoon sweet pickles, finely chopped or pickle relish
- ¼ cup 12 Bones Tomato "Q" Sauce (page 102)

This smoky and creamy dressing is extremely versatile. We like to smear this on darn near everything, but it's quite good on burgers, fried fish, and salads, and as a dipping sauce for french fries.

In a small bowl, combine all the ingredients and whisk together until combined.

BLUEBERRY-CHIPOTLE BARBECUE SAUCE

Yield: 5 cups

- 1 pound fresh or frozen blueberries
- 2 chipotle peppers in adobo sauce
- ¾ cup honey
- 3 cups 12 Bones Tomato "Q" Sauce (page 102)
- 1 teaspoon ground ginger

This is the type of sauce that gives the barbecue purists fits, but it has humble origins, even if it ended up being kind of a big deal.

Our original owner, Tom, once made this sauce for a dinner party at his own house, and everyone loved it, even though it's about as far from authentic as you get. However, when 12 Bones first opened, the barbecue aficionados turned their collective noses up at this spicy-sweet concoction.

Then, in 2007, this recipe won *Good Morning America*'s Best Bite Contest. That changed everything. "All of a sudden, it was accepted," laughs Tom. "People who tried it loved it, but it was tough convincing people that they needed to give it a try in the first place."

This sauce starts out sweet, but the finish is all chipotle. And the rich, smoky flavor ripens the longer you leave the sauce in the bottle. If you don't open it for at least a year, the smoke intensifies even further.

In a food processor or a blender, puree the berries and the chipotles. Then transfer the berry mixture to a saucepan, and add the remaining ingredients. Simmer this mixture over low heat for 30 minutes, stirring occasionally. Remove the sauce from the heat and cool.

The finished and cooled sauce can be stored in an airtight container in the refrigerator for up to a month.

SPICY VINEGAR "Q" SAUCE

Barbecue fans love to talk. A favorite—and divisive—topic among the faithful involves what type, if any, sauce belongs on smoked meat. Sauce preferences vary by region, with South Carolina sometimes throwing mustard into the mix and Kansas City preferring a heavier tomato sauce. Alabama has a white concoction with mayonnaise in it— you'll find we don't mess with that. But otherwise, we're pretty freewheeling with what goes into our own sauces. However, being that we're in North Carolina, the home of the vinegar 'cue sauce, we figured we'd incite a riot if we didn't provide some variation.

So this is our take on a tradition, kicked up and made our own with a touch of spice. This was made specifically for our pulled pork, but it can add a kick to a wide range of other dishes. You can even pour it over collard greens (page 134).

Combine all the ingredients in a saucepan on medium heat, stirring until the sugar is dissolved.

> **Note:** For the jalapeño brine, see the Jalapeño Vinegar recipe on page 118, or for a faster option, use 1 cup of juice from a jar of store-bought pickled jalapeños. We've found that the juice from Mt. Olive's pickled jalapeños will yield the closest flavor profile to our in-house recipe.

Yield: 2 quarts

- 1 quart cider vinegar
- 3 cups white vinegar
- 1 cup jalapeño brine (see note below)
- ¼ cup sugar
- 2 tablespoons garlic
- 1½ tablespoon celery salt
- 1½ tablespoon ground black pepper
- 1½ teaspoon dry English mustard
- 1¼ teaspoon red pepper flakes

SMOKED APPLE
BARBECUE SAUCE

Yield: 4 cups

6 Granny Smith apples

¼ cup, plus 1 tablespoon, brown sugar

¼ teaspoon cinnamon

1½ cups apple cider

¾ cup cider vinegar

There's likely nothing more fall-forward than this sauce: not pumpkin spice lattes, not even butternut squash soup. Apples are the true fruits of fall and, when touched with smoke, remind us of that first autumn evening when it's cold enough to fire up the woodstove.

But that doesn't mean you have to reserve it for only that time of year. This works fine for a summertime meal, slathered on ribs, pork loin, or served with super-spicy chicken wings. Or reserve it for a completely out-of-the-box Hanukkah meal, served with potato latkes.

You'll find this sauce comes out tart from the Granny Smith apples, but it ends with a mellow smokiness, a bit of sweetness from the cider, and a lingering touch of spice from the cinnamon.

Prepare a grill or smoker for 200°F indirect heat (see page 13 for more instructions on how to smoke). Then, peel, core, and slice the apples. In a medium bowl, toss the apple slices with 1 tablespoon brown sugar and the cinnamon. Place the apples in a roasting pan and smoke with heavy smoke for 1 hour at 200°F.

Once finished, combine the smoked apples with their drippings in a medium pot. Add the remaining ingredients, then bring the contents of the pot to a light boil over medium heat. Turn the heat down to low, simmer the mixture slowly for 20 minutes.

Remove the apples and puree in the food processor. Return the pureed apples to the liquid, then simmer until it has thickened to a consistency of a thin applesauce.

ingredient spotlight:
APPLES

Asheville proper has few large apple orchards, but all around the city is apple country. In the top 10 of the apple-growing states, North Carolina grows between 115 and 170 million pounds of apples on approximately 10,000 acres every year. A full 80 percent of those apples are grown in Henderson County, which is only a 20-minute drive from our south store. That's one reason you'll find apples in a couple of our desserts, as well as the Smoked Apple Barbecue Sauce on page 111.

MEMPHIS
BARBECUE SAUCE

Yield: 3 cups

- 2 cups ketchup
- ½ cup water
- 2 tablespoons balsamic vinegar
- 2 tablespoons Worcestershire sauce
- 2 tablespoons blackstrap molasses
- 1 tablespoon Gulden's spicy brown mustard
- 1½ tablespoons dark brown sugar
- 1 teaspoon granulated onion
- 1 teaspoon granulated garlic
- 1 teaspoon kosher salt
- 1 teaspoon black pepper
- 1 teaspoon red chili flakes

Memphis is basically a dry-rub city, with its focus mainly on the meat and a hands-off approach to slow smoking. If you find yourself in Memphis craving sauced-up ribs, however, you'd simply ask to have them served up "wet."

The recipe that follows is an approximation of what comes on "wet" ribs in Memphis. A tomato-based sauce that's not too heavy, not too sweet, with just the right amount of heat. Slather this on your ribs, or enjoy a squirt on a pulled pork sandwich.

Combine all ingredients in a medium saucepan and simmer on medium-low heat until heated to about 180°F.

SMOKED GARLIC BBQ SAUCE

This recipe takes the balanced flavor of Memphis Barbecue Sauce and ups the ante with sweet and smoky garlic.

    1 recipe Memphis Barbecue Sauce
    ½ cup 12 Bones Roasted Garlic (page 55)

Add both ingredients to a blender or food processor and pulse until smooth. Transfer to a saucepan and simmer until hot.

HORSERADISH
BARBECUE SAUCE

This is sort of like an Alabama White Sauce, but without the mayo. We love the bite of horseradish, and it plays well with the sweetness of the molasses and the Tomato "Q" Sauce we use in this recipe.

It makes a fine steak sauce, but we think that you'll find that it's also absolutely excellent with grilled salmon. If you don't like the heat of horseradish, just reduce the amount in the mix.

Sweat the bell pepper, onion, and garlic in the oil on low heat until soft. Whisk in the remaining ingredients, and simmer for 15 minutes.

Yield: 3 cups

- ¼ cup vegetable oil
- 1 small red bell pepper, minced
- 1 small onion, minced
- 4 cloves garlic minced
- 1¼ cup 12 Bones Tomato "Q" Sauce (page 102)
- ¼ cup Worcestershire sauce
- ½ cup prepared hot horseradish
- 1 tablespoon molasses
- 2 teaspoons coarse-ground black pepper
- 1 teaspoon cumin
- 1 teaspoon kosher salt

TANGY MUSTARD BARBECUE SAUCE

Yield: 1 quart

- 2 cups Gulden's spicy brown mustard
- ½ cup red wine vinegar
- ¼ cup balsamic vinegar
- ¼ cup light corn syrup
- 2 tablespoons Worcestershire sauce
- ¼ cup fresh lemon juice
- ½ cup water
- ⅔ cup dark brown sugar
- 2 ounces salted butter
- 1½ teaspoon cayenne

This is our take on a South Carolina mustard sauce. While it's our slowest mover of the sauces, we think that has more to do with the barbecue border wars than the flavor. Here in Western North Carolina, people like their tomato and vinegar sauces, and that's just the way it is.

This sauce has plenty to recommend it, though. For example, you don't generally think of mustard sauce as having butter and lemon juice. But that butter adds a dose of richness, while the lemon juice helps round out the mix with a touch of extra acidity. Keep in mind that because of that butter, this sauce will not have a long shelf-life. It's best to scale the recipe and make just what you need.

Simmer all the ingredients together in a medium saucepan until the butter is melted, sugar is dissolved, and sauce is smooth.

CHEERWINE
BARBECUE SAUCE

Yield: 3 cups

- 1 2-liter bottle of Cheerwine
- ½ cup sugar
- 1 cup dried sour cherries
- 1 cup 12 Bones Tomato "Q" Sauce (page 102)

This is a sweet sauce for people who love that sort of thing—and those particular folks really, really love this sauce. Since this isn't an everyday house sauce, they'll call the store to see if we have it in stock.

If you aren't familiar with Cheerwine, you likely aren't from around these parts. The original formula for this fizzy cherry soda was developed in 1917 in Salisbury, North Carolina, by a general store owner named L. D. Peeler. His great-grandson, Cliff Ritchie, runs the company today, and it's still a point of Southern pride.

As far as the flavor goes, well, we find that there is really no middle ground. Either you're obsessed with this North Carolina nectar, or you've no idea why its cult following is quite so rabidly devoted. But Cheerwine has caught on, even among bartenders, who we hear sometimes mix the sweet soda with brandy and Campari.

We have a more humble suggestion: Use it in this sweet and sticky sauce and slather it on ribs, pulled pork, and hot pepper-dusted chicken wings.

Stir together the Cheerwine and the sugar in a 3- to 4-quart, heavy-bottomed saucepan. Reduce this mixture over medium-high heat, without stirring, until it thickens enough to coat the back of a spoon. Ideally, it should resemble cough syrup, and should result in about a cup. Remove the syrup from heat and stir in the sour cherries, allowing the cherries to soften in the syrup for about 30 minutes. Stir in the water and the "Q" Sauce and transfer to a food processor or blender and puree until smooth.

JALAPEÑO "Q" SAUCE

Our most eye-catching sauce is bright green and has just a hint of sweetness, but the acidity and the peppers are the dominant components. That makes the sauce a natural on ribs and delicious with scrambled eggs.

This is a two-part recipe, which involves making a vinegar with fresh jalapeños and aromatics. The result is a spicy, flavorful brew, and we think you'll find the extra steps are worth the effort.

Do note that you'll have some Jalapeño Vinegar left over at the end of this recipe. Use it in sauces, try pickling eggs in it, or make a spicy version of the Pickled Green Tomatoes on page 151.

Puree veggies with water in a blender or a food processor. Transfer the mixture to a saucepan and add the vinegar, salt, and sugar. Simmer this on low heat just until the salt and sugar have dissolved.

Yield: 4 cups

Reserved veggies from Jalapeño Vinegar recipe (follows)

¼ cup water

1¼ cup white vinegar

1½ tablespoons kosher salt

1½ tablespoons sugar

JALAPEÑO VINEGAR

Yield: 3 cups

1 pound fresh jalapeños, stems removed (stems will make the sauce stringy but not ruin it)

1 small onion, julienned
5 cloves garlic
3 cups white vinegar

Add all ingredients to a blender or food processor and pulse until smooth. Transfer to a saucepan and simmer until hot. Cool down, then strain out the vegetables, reserving the liquid.

PINEAPPLE-HABANERO
BBQ SAUCE

After we first opened 12 Bones, we quickly realized that we were attracting a lot of spice heads who just weren't happy with a sweet sauce. We needed something to accommodate folks who wanted something with a little burn. Our Jalapeño "Q" Sauce is close, but not quite up to snuff for the obsessed. This sauce usually does the trick.

For an interesting variation on this sauce, you can also try smoking the pineapple low and slow. The caramelization of the pineapple provides extra depth. Do a big batch and try the Pineapple-Habanero Red Slaw on page 127 as well.

You can find dried habaneros at many specialty stores and Latin grocers.

Reduce the juice, chunks, and peppers in saucepan by half. Carefully puree the sauce in a blender or food processor until smooth. Return the sauce to the pan, add the 12 Bones Tomato "Q" Sauce, and simmer until hot and fully incorporated.

Yield: 3 cups

3 cups pineapple juice

1 cup pineapple chunks, drained

6 dried habaneros

1 cup 12 Bones Tomato "Q" Sauce (page 102)

HONEY-CHERRY CHIPOTLE BARBECUE SAUCE

Yield: 4-5 cups

- 2 cups Kolsch or other light-bodied beer
- 1 onion, diced
- 1 cup honey
- 1 cup dried cherries
- 2 cups 12 Bones Tomato "Q" Sauce (page 102)
- ⅓ cup chipotles, whole, in adobo sauce
- ½ cup corn syrup
- ½ cup Cheerwine
- ½ teaspoon salt
- ½ teaspoon allspice

This is a sweet barbecue sauce with mild heat. People absolutely love this at Christmas time since it's a natural pairing with family-style dishes like a whole smoked turkey (see page 86). Every year or two, we bottle this up, as well as our Cheerwine sauce on page 117, and sell them as limited-run sauces during the holidays.

In a medium saucepan, simmer the onions in the Kolsch on medium-low until soft. Add the remaining ingredients and simmer on medium-low for 20 minutes or until cherries have rehydrated. Remove from heat and puree.

PUMPKIN BARBECUE SAUCE

Yield: 5 cups

- 1 30-ounce can of pumpkin
- 2 cups 12 Bones Tomato "Q" Sauce (page 102)
- 2 cups water
- 1 teaspoon salt
- ½ teaspoon cinnamon
- ½ teaspoon coriander

This may seem like a lot of pumpkin, but it takes a lot to compete with the flavor of the Tomato "Q" Sauce. Pumpkin, by itself, really doesn't have that much flavor, but adding the cinnamon and coriander really bumps it up.

Though all our sauces are meant to go with ribs, we think this would also pair well with any cut of pork, such as chops or loin. And, even though we don't serve it at 12 Bones, this sauce would be excellent with smoked duck too.

In a medium pot, add all the ingredients and then simmer on medium heat. Stir often to prevent scorching. Remove the sauce from the heat and cool.

CRANBERRY JALAPEÑO "Q"

Yield: 4 cups

- 1 12-ounce bag of cranberries
- 1 10-ounce jar of pickled jalapeños
- 1⅓ cups of water
- ⅔ cup sugar
- 2 teaspoons lime juice
- ⅓ cup cider vinegar
- salt and pepper to taste

Want to liven up the standard leftover turkey sandwich? This is your sauce right here. We came up with this recipe right after Thanksgiving. It's a great, creative use for any leftover cranberries you might have that just didn't quite make it into the relish. It's a little tart, but it still has a fairly decent level of heat, though that can be adjusted by using fewer jalapeños in the recipe. Also try it on our smoked chicken, pork loin, or a rack of ribs (especially around holiday time). This is a much spicier version of the Cranberry Barbecue Sauce you'll find on page 92.

In a medium saucepan, add the whole cranberries, jalapeños, water, and sugar. Stir and simmer on medium-low heat until the cranberries open, about 30 minutes. Remove from the heat and puree in a food processor or blender. Add the lime juice, vinegar, and salt and pepper to taste.

V veggies, salads, and pickles

As much as folks like to think that the South is all about the meat, we like to remind them that isn't the case. Sure, we're renowned for our fried chicken and pulled pork down below the Mason-Dixon. And we can cure a ham like nobody's business. But traditional Southern tables were just as much about the vegetables, especially when produce was abundant and there wasn't much more than roots in the cellar.

Meat prices rise and fall, but historically, animal protein has been more expensive than a bunch of collards or a sack of potatoes. Those in the South knew that and were the masters of using a little meat for big flavor, even keeping what's leftover in the bottom of a pot of greens when others might throw it out. (We call that potlikker.)

Our restaurant may not be a huge destination for vegetarians, but we know that they're coming in. If we take the cucumber salad or marinated portobellos off the menu, we hear a lot about it. But for those who miss the cuke salad come winter, we have a variety of other sides, including some heartier, cold-weather fare. We try to keep things fresh and interesting year round, so that the plates of four sides are (almost) as good a meal as the plates with meat.

SWEET VINEGAR
COLESLAW

This recipe has actually been passed down through the family of our founder, Sabra, which means this is a real Southern heirloom. It's the perfect side for a plate of 'cue and adds an often-needed shot of vegetables. And this slaw is free of mayonnaise, which makes it a bit healthier than others.

True, the slaw calls for a decent amount of sugar, but the sweetness is tamed by the addition of the cider vinegar. While this recipe lists pre-shredded cabbage, feel free to pass one to two heads of green cabbage through the shredding attachment of a food processor. Just make sure it's nice and fine. If you can't find celery seed, use celery salt to taste, and don't use the additional salt this recipe calls for.

Combine the sugar, oil, vinegar, celery seed, salt, and pepper in a 4- to 6-quart stockpot. Bring the vinegar mixture to a boil while stirring to dissolve the sugar. As soon as the liquid begins to boil, reduce the heat to medium. Next, add the sliced onion. Stir and cook for 1 minute. Add the green bell pepper, stir, and cook for an additional minute. Remove the mixture from the heat and combine the hot liquid with the cabbage and carrots in a large mixing bowl. Once the cabbage has wilted, the slaw is ready to cool in the refrigerator. Check your seasonings and adjust to suit your taste. For a deeper flavor, let the slaw marinate in the refrigerator overnight.

Yield: About 6–8 servings

- ¾ cup sugar
- ¾ cup vegetable oil or mild olive oil
- ¾ cup cider vinegar
- 2 teaspoons celery seed
- 2 teaspoons kosher salt
- 2 teaspoons coarse-ground black pepper
- 1 medium yellow onion, julienned
- 1 medium green bell pepper, julienned
- 2 1-pound bags of shredded cabbage
- 1 medium carrot, peeled and shredded

PINEAPPLE-HABANERO
RED SLAW

Yield: 8 servings

- 1 26-ounce can of pineapple chunks with juice
- 2 pounds red cabbage, shredded
- 2 medium carrots, shredded
- 1 cup mayonnaise
- 1 tablespoon brown sugar
- 2 tablespoons Pineapple-Habanero BBQ Sauce (page 120)

  Salt and pepper to taste (use smoked sea salt for an extra smoky kick)

This is what we sometimes have on hand for those customers who simply must have mayonnaise in their coleslaw. Contrary to what you might think from the name, it's only mildly spicy, tempered by the addition of mayo. If you want to skip smoking the pineapple, that's fine. It will change the flavor a bit, but you'll still get the essence of the fruit.

Reserve juice from pineapple chunks and spread pineapple evenly on a baking pan. Smoke at 200° F for 1 hour or roast in oven at 350° F for 1 hour. Let chunks cool with pineapple juice. In a medium mixing bowl, add all ingredients and combine well. Allow to rest until cabbage is semi-soft. For best results, make a day ahead of serving.

CUCUMBER SALAD

Besides fresh, sliced tomatoes, nothing quite says summer like cucumbers. But the thing about cucumbers is that it seems like once they start filling up the garden, they just don't quit. And there are only so many pickles you can make and eat (see recipes starting on page 151 for more pickle ideas).

One solution to the cucumber surplus is salad, tossed with summer tomatoes, sweet onions, and salty feta cheese. This will be the hit of any summer backyard barbecue, when people begin craving things like watermelon and anything else they can think of to help cool down. At 12 Bones, we serve this to people who have slaw fatigue, but are still looking for something fresh and crisp to eat with their pulled pork platters.

Combine all the vinaigrette ingredients in a blender or a food processor and blend until they are fully emulsified. Any leftover dressing can be kept for two weeks in an airtight container or used in the recipe for pickled okra salad (see page 152).

Peel four strips of skin off of each cucumber lengthwise with a sharp peeler. Halve the cucumbers lengthwise, and then gently scoop out the seeds with a spoon. Slice the cucumbers crosswise in a 1/8-inch thick bias cut. Toss the slices with remaining ingredients in a bowl and chill for at least 1 hour. This salad holds, refrigerated, for up to three days.

Yield: 10-12 servings

For the vinaigrette (makes 3 cups):

- 2 cups red wine vinegar
- 1/4 cup vegetable oil
- 3 tablespoons light corn syrup
- 2 tablespoons Gulden's spicy brown mustard
- 3 tablespoons pesto
- 3 tablespoons dark brown sugar
- 1 teaspoon kosher salt
- 1/2 teaspoon red pepper flakes
- 1/2 teaspoon dried basil
- 1/2 teaspoon dried oregano
- 1/2 teaspoon dried thyme

For the salad:

- 8 large English cucumbers
- 5 small Roma tomatoes, julienned
- 1 small red or sweet yellow onion, julienned
- 1/2 cup crumbled feta cheese
- 2 cups cucumber vinaigrette

12 BONES WEDGE SALAD

Yield: 4 servings

For the onion strings:

1 cup all-purpose flour

1 tablespoon 12 Bones Chicken Rub (page 26)

1 yellow onion, sliced thin

   oil

For the salad:

1 head iceberg lettuce

2 tomatoes, cut into 4 wedges each

8 slices cucumber, for garnish

1 recipe Spicy Ranch Dressing (follows, or use store-bought dressing)

4 slices of cooked 12 Bones Brown Sugar Bacon (page 41), or substitute plain cooked bacon, chopped

1 recipe Onion Strings (above)

The Wedge Salad enjoyed a heyday in the '50s and '60s, but fell out of favor in the '70s, replaced by more interesting and nutritionally wholesome greens. By the '90s, iceberg lettuce was frequently relegated to taco bars and fast food hamburgers.

Unfailingly retro, but popular by merit of its ability to be both a salad and comfort food at the same time, the iceberg wedge is staging a strong comeback. Our Wedge Salad is a nod to the classic with our own little twists. We make our own ranch dressing and spike it with chipotle peppers, then we pile a mess of fried onion strings over the top for good measure.

To make the onion strings, whisk together the flour and the chicken rub. Slice the onions as thinly as possible, roughly the width of spaghetti. Dip the onion strings in the water, then shake off the excess liquid. Dredge the onion slices in the seasoned flour, being sure to coat each string. Shake off the excess flour, and fry the onion rings in 350°F oil until they turn golden brown. Turn halfway through the cooking process using metal or wooden tongs.

Be careful: These strings cook quickly, in about 30 to 45 seconds. They'll go from perfect to burnt in seconds. Once they're ready, remove them from the oil and drain them on a baking sheet atop a clean, dry paper towel.

To make the salad, cut the lettuce into four wedges. Put each wedge on a plate or in a salad bowl. Garnish each lettuce wedge with two tomato wedges and two slices of cucumber. Then dress each lettuce wedge with one-fourth of the dressing. Finish with bacon crumbles and onion strings. Serve immediately.

SPICY RANCH DRESSING

<u>Yields: 1½ cups, enough for four salads.</u>

½ cup sour cream
⅓ cup mayonnaise
1 teaspoon granulated garlic
1 teaspoon granulated onion
1 teaspoon dried oregano

1 teaspoon salt
1 chipotle pepper in adobo sauce,
  depending on heat desired
⅓ cup buttermilk

Pulse all the ingredients, except buttermilk, in a food processor or blender until the mixture resembles Thousand Island dressing. Stop the processor and scrape down the sides. Start the processor again, and add the buttermilk. Stop and scrape. Pulse one more time.

Store any leftovers in an airtight container.

RED CABBAGE
SAUERKRAUT

Red kraut, also known as ruby kraut, is full of vitamin C (much more so than its more pallid cousin). Though some krauts are fermented, this is more of a quick-style version, which is designed to be just as good as the more pungent stuff you'll find piled on hot dogs, sausages, or a stacked pork sandwich.

At 12 Bones, we use this on our Reuben (page 67), and we also think it's delicious on the side of the 12 Bones Bratwurst (page 44) with a scoop of potato salad.

In a small stockpot, heat the oil over medium-high heat and sauté the onions. Add the red cabbage and sweat for 2 minutes. Add the cider vinegar, salt, and caraway seed. Bring to a boil for 1 minute. Stir to coat and mix cabbage and onion. Remove from heat and cool for 24 hours in order to let the flavor really soak in.

Yield: about 6 1-cup servings

- 1 tablespoon vegetable oil
- 1 medium onion, julienned
- 2 pounds red cabbage, shredded
- 1⅓ cups cider vinegar
- 1 tablespoon kosher salt
- 1½ teaspoons caraway seed

SIMPLE GREEN SALAD
WITH ROASTED TOMATO
VINAIGRETTE

Yield: 1½ cups

To make the dressing:

3   Roma tomatoes

⅓ cup vegetable oil, plus
    1 tablespoon

2   tablespoons cider vinegar

2   tablespoons pesto

¼ tablespoon sugar

¼ tablespoon dry
    English mustard

½ teaspoon
    Worcestershire sauce

½ teaspoon kosher salt

This vinaigrette will dress up a tasty salad for a crowd. At 12 Bones, we toss it with mixed baby greens, dried cherries, toasted pecans, cucumbers, feta cheese, and sliced tomatoes. However, it also makes a nice substitution on the 12 Bones Wedge Salad (page 130).

Preheat the oven to 375°F. Core and halve the tomatoes lengthwise, then toss with 1 tablespoon of oil. Roast the tomatoes, skin side up, on a baking pan in the oven for 10 minutes. Remove from oven and take off the skins while still warm. Add the tomatoes to a blender or food processor, along with the remaining ingredients, and blend.

Put salad mix of your choice in a large mixing bowl, lightly season with salt and pepper, and toss with enough dressing to suit your taste. Garnish the salad with nuts, cheese, or vegetables of your choice. Unused dressing will keep up to five days, covered and refrigerated.

COLLARD GREENS

A mess of greens, stewed with a chunk of fatback, is a time-honored ode to home-style cooking. This recipe doesn't call for it, but providing a bottle of hot sauce is always a good idea with these porky greens. We like Texas Pete.

At 12 Bones, we go through 360 pounds of collard greens a week, give or take. Obviously, our greens have earned us more than a few fans. Just ask Gary and Darla Dodd, longtime 12 Bones regulars. So strong is Darla's devotion to our food, she created a little jingle: "I'm so glad I'm from the South, with 12 Bones collards and ribs in my mouth."

Per the ditty, Darla and Gary are Southerners through and through. Darla is from Greensboro, which is two and a half hours east of Asheville. Gary, a local trial lawyer, went to law school in Knoxville, Tennessee. "We've eaten in a lot of soul food restaurants, all around," says Darla. "And we prefer this over any soul food restaurant we've eaten."

Is 12 Bones soul food? "It really is soul food, because it has those home-cooked collards," Darla says emphatically. "I'm telling you, they go to a lot of trouble. They put bacon and butter in there, I don't know what all, but they cook those collards forever and they are just heavenly."

Yield: 4–6 servings

- 3 tablespoons bacon fat or butter
- 8 ounces bacon, diced (or leave this out for the vegetarians and adjust the seasoning)
- 2 yellow onions, julienned
- 2 pounds collard greens, divided and triple rinsed, large parts of stem trimmed
- 2 tablespoons dark brown sugar
- 2½ teaspoons kosher salt
- 1½ teaspoons coarse-ground black pepper
- 2 cups stock

Add bacon fat or butter and bacon to a heavy-bottomed 6- to 8-quart stockpot. Cook over medium heat, stirring with a wooden spoon, until the fat renders out and the bacon gets crispy. Add the onions to the rendered fat in the stockpot, and sweat until they go soft, taking care not to brown them. Add half of the greens to the pot and stir, being sure to keep them from sticking to the bottom. Stir in the seasonings and the remaining greens. Pour in the stock, stir the pot some more, and then cover it. Reduce the heat to medium-low, and simmer the greens until the stems are no longer stringy but not mushy. Stir greens every 5 minutes or so.

Cooking time will vary, depending on whether you use precut or fresh collard greens. No matter what, this will take some time, but it will be well worth it. Adjust seasonings as desired right before serving.

ingredient spotlight:
COLLARD GREENS

Collards are said to bring good luck in the New Year and are traditionally consumed with black-eyed peas for an extra punch of good fortune. Historically, collards manifested luck in more practical ways too. Before the time of modern grocery stores, with their fluorescent-lit rows of fruits and vegetables available year-round, not much was growing in the dead of winter. But the hearty collard is quite cold tolerant and, with proper care, could offer sustenance year-round.

Particularly in the Southeast, collards are fairly easy to find in the produce section of the grocery store. If your store doesn't carry whole bunches, look for cleaned and chopped packaged mixes in the bagged salad section. There's no shame in it.

Furthermore, if you're using whole, bunched collards, make sure to soak them in several different changes of fresh, cold water. Sand can easily cling to the leaves and stems—and no one likes grit in their greens.

To cut whole collards, trim the woody parts of the stems (some like to remove the stems altogether; if you do this, reduce your cooking time). After trimming, layer several leaves of cleaned and drained collards on top of each other, then roll the bundle into a cigar shape. Slice down the cigar, an inch at a time, to cut all the greens into approximately the same size.

BLACK BEAN SALAD

Yield: 4 servings

- 1 15-ounce can of black beans
- 2½ cups of corn kernels
- 2 small Roma tomatoes, diced
- 1 poblano pepper, diced
- 2 tablespoons chopped cilantro (or more to taste)
- 1 stalk celery, diced
- 4 scallions, sliced
- 1 tablespoon Gulden's spicy brown mustard
- ½ cup Cucumber Vinaigrette (page 128) or substitute high-quality Italian-style dressing; we like Newman's oil and vinegar
- 1 teaspoon salt
- 1 teaspoon ground cumin
- ½ teaspoon ground black pepper

This started out as a pinto bean salad, and it wasn't a huge hit. But once we replaced the pintos with black beans, it flew out of the kitchen. It might have helped that we called it Texas Caviar, since it was our riff on that classic dish with black-eyed peas. We're full of contradictions at 12 Bones.

Carefully rinse the black beans, trying not to break or crush them. Allow them to drain dry, and then set them aside. Smoke the corn in heavy smoke on a sheet pan at 200°F for 45 minutes. See page 13 for smoking tips.

Meanwhile, combine the tomatoes, poblano pepper, cilantro, celery, and scallion in a large mixing bowl. Add mustard, vinaigrette, and spices. Gently mix black beans into this mixture, taste, and adjust seasoning.

SUCCOTASH

People love this succotash. It's also one of our lighter dishes—or at least it doesn't have any bacon fat. The origin of this dish is very, very old. Its name comes from a Native American word for "broken corn," and it's likely early American settlers learned how to make this dish upon arrival to America. Original recipes for succotash are long lost, but we know they bore only a passing resemblance to what we usually serve on our Thanksgiving tables (or the shriveled version that kids are forced to eat in the school cafeteria). Original recipes included items that rarely make it into today's succotash pot: bear fat, fish, and wild roots, for example. What this version has to recommend it is the fact that it's a fairly quick dish, and you don't have to source even a tablespoon of bear fat to make it taste good.

Melt the butter over medium heat in a large skillet or a medium saucepan. Add the onion and the garlic, then cook for 2 minutes while stirring. Next, add the stock and the allspice. Cook and stir until almost dry. Add the beans and the corn. Cover and reduce the heat to low, and simmer for about 10 minutes, or until the beans are tender, stirring occasionally. Remove from the heat, then stir in the cilantro. Season to taste with salt and pepper.

Yield: 6–8 servings

- 2 ounces of butter
- 1 small onion, minced
- 4 cloves garlic, chopped
- 1 cup of chicken or pork stock (or vegetable stock)
- ½ teaspoon ground allspice
- 1 1-pound bag of frozen lima beans
- 2½ cups frozen corn kernels
- 2 tablespoons chopped cilantro

  Salt and pepper to taste

BUTTERED GREEN BEANS

Yield: 6–8 servings

6 ounces salted butter

10 cloves fresh garlic, minced

4 pounds frozen cut green beans

4 teaspoons kosher salt

2 teaspoons ground black pepper

Some may question the inclusion of frozen beans in this recipe. However, there's a reason in a restaurant like ours—where nearly everything is fresh—that we prefer frozen beans most of the year. Good-quality frozen beans are better tasting than out-of-season green beans or green beans flown halfway around the world. Try to find flash-frozen beans for best quality.

Of course, when the green beans are heavy on the vine, by all means adapt this recipe to suit your overabundance. Simply remove the fibrous string from your beans, chop them into approximately 1-inch pieces, blanch them in boiling water until just green, and then shock them in ice-cold water to stop the cooking process. Then proceed with this recipe.

Melt the butter in a heavy-bottomed stockpot on medium heat. Add the garlic and sauté until golden brown, stirring constantly. Add the green beans, salt, and pepper, and stir. Be sure to scrape the bottom of the pot to prevent the garlic from burning. Cook the beans until they are tender, stirring occasionally.

SMOKY TOMATO
BASIL SOUP

Most soups are amazing in the winter, and this is no exception. The smoky flavor adds a depth that's far beyond your average can of pre-made soup. Still, it's often the case that better basil can be found during the summer. That's an unfortunate circumstance, because we don't recommend substituting dried basil for fresh. Nothing beats fresh basil, so do your best to find it, no matter the season.

Many people are surprised to hear that we serve soup at a smokehouse known mostly for its meat. While we serve this as a side (meaning you don't have to forego your ribs, if you don't want), we also serve it up as a meal in itself, with a hunk of our Cheddar-Jalapeño Cornbread. Add a salad, if you want, for a more complete meal.

Preheat oven, grill, or smoker to 300°F. Core and cut the tomatoes in half, lengthwise. Toss them with just enough vegetable oil to coat. Roast or smoke the tomatoes, skin side up, for 15 minutes. Remove the skin while the tomatoes are still hot. Melt the butter in a medium pot. Add the onion and garlic, and sweat on low heat until soft. Add the tomatoes and the remaining ingredients except for the cream and Parmesan to the pot, and cook on medium heat for 30 minutes. Add the cream and Parmesan and remove from the heat. Stir until the Parmesan has melted. Taste for seasoning. Transfer the soup to a food processor, or blender, or use a stick blender to puree until smooth.

Yield: 4 servings

- 12 Roma tomatoes
- 1 tablespoon vegetable oil
- 2 tablespoons butter
- 1 yellow onion, diced
- 4 cloves chopped garlic
- 1 14-ounce can tomatoes in juice
- 2 cups 12 Bones Pork Stock (page 59) or store-bought chicken stock
- 2 tablespoons Worcestershire sauce
- 1 tablespoon Cholula brand hot sauce
- 1 tablespoon 12 Bones Chicken Rub (page 26)
- 1 teaspoon salt
- 1 teaspoon black pepper
- ¼ cup fresh basil (stems removed and rough chopped)
- 2 tablespoons sugar
- 1 cup heavy cream
- ½ cup Parmesan, grated

CROCKPOT
PINTO BEANS

Yield: Up to 12 servings

1   1-pound bag of dried
    pinto beans

    Water

1   smoked ham hock

    Salt and pepper to taste

This is a great recipe for those too busy to put a whole lot of fuss in their food—or for those times you need something that can take care of itself on the back burner. There's just not much you need to do with a pot of beans, some salt and pepper, and a ham hock.

What is a ham hock, you ask? It's essentially a cut of meat culled from the fatty bit that makes up the lower shank of a pig's leg. A soul food standard, a ham hock is neither ankle nor foot, but not part of the ham either. It's a mass of tendon and ligament with a touch of meat. In some places, particularly the South, it's easy to find them in the grocery store, already smoked and ready to lend flavor and body to your beans or what have you.

Note: It's important not to presoak the beans for this recipe, or they will be done before the ham hock is tender and has released all its collagen. Also, make sure not to add salt until the beans are fully cooked. The ham hock will likely have enough salt to season the beans, so be sure to taste before adding any additional seasoning.

Empty the bag of beans into the crockpot and cover with cold water. Give the beans and water a stir. Discard any beans that float, and then drain the water. Place the ham hock in the center of the beans, making sure that the cut side is facing down and that no beans are under it. Add enough cold water to cover the beans by 4 inches. Cook the beans, covered, on low for about 4 hours. Stir, then cook until the beans are tender but not falling apart, about another 2 hours. The total time depends on your crockpot. Taste and adjust the seasonings.

PORTOBELLO MUSHROOMS

Living in Asheville, North Carolina, there are plenty of vegetarians among our friends and customers. That's why we treat our portobello mushrooms much like we would anything else—with tender, loving care. We marinate the caps with plenty of spices and flavors, pat them dry, and give them a good, long smoke. Then we layer them with pesto mayo (page 91), fried green tomatoes (page 148), and lettuce on good, crusty wheat bread.

You don't have to make a sandwich with these, of course. They're very nice wrapped in a tortilla with rice and beans, or sliced and fanned out on a fresh, summer salad. There's no end to what you can do with these 'shrooms. Just remember that your vegetarian friends would prefer that you cook them where they won't come into contact with any meat.

To make the marinade, pulse all ingredients in a food processor until smooth.

To make the mushrooms, remove the stems of about 12 mushrooms and wipe away any dirt (instead of rinsing them). Mushrooms absorb liquid quickly, so you'll want to make sure they're not so full of water that they can't take in as much of the delicious marinade you've made.

To prepare the mushrooms for roasting, dip them one at a time in the marinade. Then place them, top-down, on a roasting pan if you're planning to roast them in the oven. Or place them directly on a roasting rack if you're planning to smoke them. Spoon extra marinade into the cap before cooking. See page 13 for tips on smoking. Smoke or roast at 245°F for 30 minutes or until tender.

Yield: Good for at least 6 servings

12 portobello mushrooms

For the marinade:

2 cups balsamic vinegar

1½ cups vegetable oil

2 tablespoons Gulden's spicy brown mustard

1 small yellow onion, chopped

2 garlic cloves

¼ cup dark brown sugar

1 tablespoon coarse-ground black pepper

1 tablespoon kosher salt

STAY FRESH BUTT

NiNE MiLE

EPSILON
Built for the Mountain Life
mountainbikihabs.com

Mama's Little YELLA PILS

Gravity Sh

SHOW US YOUR GR
WWW.GRITTYS.CO

, fast pig

HOGZILL

SPECIAL TODAY

Special Side
Mushroom + Sausage
Cass. $1.75

Special Dessert
Peanutbutter + Banana
Upside Down Cake
$3.50

ORGANIC

BASK
AK + BK
Sept 7 2013

TRIDE BURST

DES MOINES:
HELL YES.

SPECIALS

TELIC

TODAYS
★RIB FLAVORS★

BROWN SUGAR ★DRY RUB★
"NEKKID" ★SALT & PEPPER DRY RUB★
BLUEBERRY

sides for the:
EXTENDED
FAMILY

Darla and Gary Dodd tend to come by on Fridays, usually between 3 and 3:30, and they always try to sit in the same place. Besides those ribs and collards, they're pretty partial to the corn pudding. "There's nothing in the world better than that corn pudding," says Darla.

If we happen to be running low on corn pudding, we'll set some aside for the Dodds. Rest assured, we don't do that for everyone. And every time Chef Shane makes an extra special dessert, he'll save a little something for them too. "Shane makes such delicious desserts that it's unbelievable," Darla says. Once in a while, we'll even give them a whole Christmas pie. The Dodds are also generous: At Christmastime, they always give the staff extra tips.

"They're like a family there," says Darla. "They really are. And they're so genuine. I really feel so privileged to live where I can get such wonderful food and be around such wonderful people. I would be really disappointed if I couldn't get there on a regular basis."

FRIED GREEN
TOMATOES

Lately, fried green tomatoes have become en vogue in restaurants all over the country, thanks in part to the countrywide popularity of Southern cuisine. Though a goodly number of restaurants in New York City lay claim to their own versions—some even slapping them on pizza— you know, as they do, the heart of this dish belongs to the South.

We serve our Fried Green Tomatoes on a vegetarian sandwich with bright, herbaceous mayo and smoky portobello mushrooms (page 144). We also put them on our BLT, or serve them at parties with our Spicy Ranch Dressing (page 131) as a dipping sauce.

This recipe calls for seasoning the tomato batter with 12 Bones Chicken Rub, but you can use any kind of seasoning salt you might prefer. Just make sure to adjust the recipe to suit the salt level of whatever seasoning you choose, but don't skimp; green tomatoes need a bit of help to shine. You can double, triple, or quadruple this recipe to feed a crowd.

Yield: About 6 slices, enough for two sandwiches.

1   cup all-purpose flour

2   tablespoons 12 Bones Chicken Rub (page 26)

1   cup cornmeal
    vegetable oil

1   egg

¼   cup buttermilk

1   green tomato, cored and sliced to ⅛-to ¼ -inch thickness

To make the breading, in a small mixing bowl, whisk together the flour and half of the Chicken Rub. Pour onto a dinner plate or a platter. In the same bowl, whisk together the cornmeal with the rest of the Chicken Rub. Pour onto a separate plate or platter and set aside.

Whisk together the egg and the buttermilk in a bowl or shallow dish until smooth. Dust the flour mixture onto a tomato slice, then dip the slice in the buttermilk mixture until fully wet. Then dredge the slice in the cornmeal mixture, and shake off the excess. Try to use one hand to handle the dry ingredients and another hand to handle the wet ingredients.

Repeat this process with the remaining slices, setting each aside on a clean plate. Then, deep-fry the tomatoes in vegetable oil, heated to 350°F, until golden. Place the tomatoes on a paper towel to drain off the oil, and serve while still hot.

HOW TO **PICKLE**

Pickling predates refrigeration and is one preservation technique that's stood the test of time, particularly in the South. In the grocery store aisle, "pickle" tends to be a noun. In those air-conditioned and fluorescent-lit spaces, a pickle is a brined cucumber in spears, chips, or slices. In other, better-lit places, "pickle" is a verb, and it means to preserve something in brine, often with vinegar.

In the American South in particular, vast treatises have been written on the virtues of pickling. Down here, we'll brine nearly anything. Pickled eggs line our bar shelves. Pickled pig's feet? We've got 'em. Heck, we'll even pickle fruit to preserve it past the season's peak.

We will, as our grandmothers and grandfathers have before us, put up all manner of things green and growing when the season is on and the produce is plentiful. Pickled vegetables can include beets, peppers, tomatoes (green, preferably), okra and, of course, cucumbers. Many a Southern home gardener grows prickly, knobby cucumbers specifically for that purpose. And we're better for it come the wintertime, when garden produce is a distant memory.

Pickles are equally at home on cold appetizer platters, salads, and sandwiches. Or chop the pickles on the following pages into bits, add a touch of chopped onion, and you have yourself a fine relish.

If you prepare the recipes on the next few pages, you can pour them into clean jars and keep them around in the refrigerator for a few weeks, max. If you'd like to extend the life of your pickles, you'll want to learn how to process them in a boiling water bath.

You can purchase a boiling water bath canner, or you can easily create one out of a large pot with a lid and a rack that keeps the bottoms of the jars from coming into contact with the bottom of the pot, which should be big enough to hold your jars, allow for the water to cover them by about an inch or so, and not overflow while the water is boiling.

Once you've got that all figured out, you'll need some pickling jars. Most every grocery store carries boxes of Ball jars, plus the lids and bands. Make sure the jars are free of nicks and chips, which might cause improper sealing. Wash the jars in hot, soapy water, and rinse well. Next, heat the jars and lids in a barely simmering hot water bath in a stockpot, and keep them hot until you're ready to use them.

Prepare your pickle recipe and pour it into your hot jars and seal them, leaving a ½-inch headspace between the pickles and the lid. Wipe any residue from the rim with a clean towel. Now, it's time to process your pickles.

Place the sealed and cleaned jars in a boiling water bath. Add enough water to cover the jars by 1 to 2 inches. Next, bring the water back to a gently rolling boil, and let the jars sit in the boiling water for the time specified in the recipe.

Using tongs, remove the jars from the water bath when the time is up. Place them right side up on several towels, leaving space between each jar. Let them cool. The center of the lid should not flex when you press it. Store your pickles in your pantry or cabinets. The flavor of pickles will develop over time.

PICKLED GREEN TOMATOES

Yield: 1 quart

- ¾ cup water
- ¾ cup cider vinegar
- 1 tablespoon kosher salt
- 2 teaspoons sugar
- 1 teaspoon crushed black peppercorns
- 3 cloves garlic, crushed
- ½ teaspoon red chili flakes
- ½ teaspoon whole coriander
- 1 pound green tomatoes, cleaned, cored, and sliced ¼ -inch thick

Southerners like to claim they were the first to think up recipes for green tomatoes. But tomato gardeners in every corner of the world, at least the ones where they grow, know that late-season fruit sometimes gets big and swollen on the vine but never gets quite enough heat and sun to turn sweet. Especially at the tail end of an abundant harvest, it's easy to think that our garden will continue to bear fruit indefinitely. But the first frost is a swift reminder of the impermanence of the growing season. Instead of letting green tomatoes go to waste, try preserving them. (If you'd rather fry them, that's fine too. See our recipe on page 148.) Pickled green tomatoes are a great way to preserve fruit for a time when no tomatoes, green or otherwise, remain.

In a nonreactive saucepan, combine all the ingredients, except for the tomatoes, to make the pickling liquid. Bring the pickling liquid to a boil, stirring all the while to dissolve the salt and the sugar. Remove this mixture from the heat and cool down to room temperature.

Place the tomatoes in a clean, 1-quart glass jar and pour the pickling liquid over the tomatoes to within ½ inch of the top. Seal the jar, then process in a boiling water bath for 10 minutes to preserve, or place it in the refrigerator to chill for at least 6 hours before eating.

Note: For spicy pickled green tomatoes, replace the cider vinegar with the Jalapeño Vinegar on page 118.

PICKLED OKRA

Okra is especially prolific in the South during the long, hot days of late summer. Here in Western North Carolina, you're likely to find pickled okra in your Bloody Mary, and sometimes even served alongside your sandwich in lieu of a dill pickle spear. If you're a gardener, this pickle recipe is a great use of the summer's bounty. Make sure to check out our Pickled Okra Salad recipe (below) as well.

Pack the cleaned and trimmed okra into four clean quart jars. In a medium saucepan, combine the vinegar, water, salt, and sugar. Simmer over low heat, until the sugar and the salt is dissolved. In a small mixing bowl, stir together the mustard seeds, the coriander, pepper flakes, and the peppercorns. Divide the spices between the jars, and place two garlic cloves in each jar. Pour hot pickling liquid over the okra leaving at least ½ inch headspace at the top. Remove air bubbles, seal, and process in a hot water bath for 15 minutes.

Yield: 4 quarts

- 1 pound fresh okra, rinsed and stem trimmed to ¼ inch
- 2 cups cider vinegar
- 2 cups water
- 3 tablespoons salt
- 1 tablespoon sugar
- 2 tablespoons mustard seed
- 1 tablespoon whole coriander seeds
- 1 tablespoon red pepper flakes
- 1 tablespoon whole black peppercorns
- 8 cloves garlic, peeled

PICKLED OKRA SALAD

Yield: 5 cups
4 cups pickled okra, drained (about 16 pieces)
1 small yellow onion, diced
1 poblano, stem and seeds removed, julienned
2 Roma tomatoes, julienned
½ cup cucumber vinaigrette (page 128, or substitute vinaigrette of your choice)

This is a good use for pickled okra—that's assuming you can manage to keep it around. This is another side that works for meat-eaters and vegetarians alike. At 12 Bones, we find that both sides of the meat debate enjoy this dish. Many like it as a crisp foil to our pulled pork, while others think its acidity cuts through rich mac and cheese nicely.

Slice okra in half, lengthwise, and toss with the remaining ingredients. Marinate overnight.

GRANDPA BUCK'S
PICKLED
RED BEETS

A treat from Bryan's side of the family, these pickles come from his grandfather, Buck. Buck had a full half-acre garden at his Hickory homestead, and a visit always included checking out the largest ripe fruits and vegetables. While a half-acre might seem like a large garden, Buck grew up on a tobacco farm with even larger acreage and also co-owned a milk distributing business. A half-acre was just a hobby garden for him. With such a large kitchen garden, it was inevitable that much of the produce would find its way into preserves and pickles. These beets are one of his favorite quick recipes (and ours too).

Yield: 1 quart

1 pound beets, cleaned and trimmed, leaving ¼ - to ½ -inch stem

⅓ cup water

⅓ cup sugar

⅓ cup cider vinegar

Rinse dirt from beets. Trim the beets to leave a ¼- to ½-inch stem, then place them in a large saucepan with enough water to cover them. Bring the beets to a boil and then cook until tender (check with a fork or a knife). Beets should be firm, not soft and mushy.

After boiling put the boiled beets in cold water, and let them cool until you can handle them comfortably. Meanwhile, in another saucepan, combine the remaining ingredients and boil the pickling mixture. Once the beets have cooled, use a towel to gently rub off the skins.

Slice or quarter beets and put them in 1-quart canning jars. Pour heated brine over beets, being sure not to fill juice to top of jar—leave at least ½ inch of space. Screw on the lid and seal. Process in a hot water bath for 30 minutes, or cool and keep for several weeks, refrigerated.

Allow at least 1 to 2 days to pickle before serving.

AUNT VIOLET'S MUSTARD PICKLES

This is an old recipe, courtesy of a true Southern belle: Bryan's Great Aunt Violet. Bryan says he can still remember her awe-inspiring kitchen. Since cooking for family and friends was her passion, there was always something interesting on the stove or in the oven. We could always expect homemade pies and cakes or other creations made from her garden. She was particularly well-known for these mustard pickles. The base recipe is similar to a typical sweet bread-and-butter–style pickle, but the mustard helps cut through the sugar and adds an unusual complexity.

Slice cucumbers horizontally, about ¼-inch thick. Set aside. In a large saucepan, bring the water, sugar, and cider vinegar to a boil, and then add the cucumbers and cook until the color changes. Put the yellow mustard, red pepper flakes, and salt in the bottom of the jar. Pour the cucumbers and brine into the jar, leaving a ¼-inch headroom. Screw on the lid and seal. Shake the jar when it cools to incorporate the mustard into the brine. Ultimately, the mustard will clump, but shaking it does help. Let the pickles come to room temperature, and then store them in the refrigerator for 1 to 2 weeks. Allow at least 1 to 2 days to pickle before serving.

Yield: 1 quart

- 1 pound cucumbers, about 2–3 medium to large size
- ⅓ cup water
- ⅓ cup sugar
- ⅓ cup cider vinegar
- 1 tablespoon yellow table mustard
- 1 teaspoon red pepper flakes
- 1 teaspoon, or up to ½ tablespoon kosher salt (depending on taste)

PICKLED
CANTALOUPE

Yield: 1 quart

¾ cup white vinegar

½ cup water

1 cinnamon stick

½ teaspoon whole cloves

½ teaspoon whole allspice

¼ teaspoon fresh nutmeg

1 cup sugar

1 large cantaloupe, peeled, seeded, and cut into 1-inch cubes or balled

Every gardener with a prolific melon patch knows that when cantaloupe ripens, it often seems like it's all at once. Instead of getting overwhelmed by the impermanence of it all, try pickling what you don't think you can manage to eat. When it's full-on winter, you'll be happy you did. For those of you who don't have a garden, you likely know the frustration of cutting open a melon, only to find it's not completely ripe. Don't throw that green melon away. This recipe is for you.

Combine the vinegar and the water in a large saucepan. Tie the spices in a spice bag or a piece of cheesecloth, and add the bundle to the pan. Bring the mixture to a boil, and then reduce the heat to low and simmer for about 5 minutes. Remove the mixture from the heat, cover, and steep at room temperature for about 1 hour. Remove the spice bag, then return the pan to the stove and add the sugar. Stir over medium heat until the sugar has dissolved.

For refrigerator pickles, remove from the heat and add the melon. Place a heat-proof plate on top of the melon to keep it submerged. Steep until the pickled melon mixture reaches room temperature. Remove the plate, cover, and chill for at least 2 hours and up to five days.

For longer-lasting pickles, place the pickles in a 1-quart, sterilized jar, per instructions on page 150. Pour the hot pickling liquid over the cantaloupe and process in a hot water bath for 15 minutes.

WATERMELON RIND PICKLES

Sure, the vast majority of people toss watermelon rind in the garbage. What a shame. These pickles, sweet, tart, and full of spices and a touch of summer herbs, are a wonderful treat.

Cover the melon rind with salt and 2 quarts of the water, then stir to dissolve. Let the mixture stand for at least 4 hours or up to 12 hours. Drain and rinse the melon. Cover melon with the remaining water in a large saucepan and simmer over low heat until just tender, about 30 minutes. Drain and set aside. Tie the cinnamon, cloves, allspice, and mustard seeds in a spice bag or a piece of cheesecloth. Combine the spice bag, sugar, mint, and vinegar in a large saucepan and bring to a boil. Reduce the heat and simmer for 10 minutes. Add the melon and simmer for an additional 10 minutes.

If canning, pack the hot watermelon rind into sterilized pint jars and cover with hot syrup, leaving ½-inch headspace, and seal with clean lids. Process the jars in a hot water bath for 15 minutes. Remove jars and let them sit undisturbed at room temperature for 24 hours.

If not canning, remove the melon from the heat and then let stand until it's cooled to room temperature. Transfer to a nonreactive container, cover, and chill for at least 12 hours and for up to two weeks.

Yield: 5–7 pints

- 2 quarts watermelon rind cut into 1-inch cubes (white parts only, about one medium-size melon)
- ½ cup pickling salt
- 1 gallon water, divided
- 2 cinnamon sticks
- 1 tablespoon whole cloves
- 1 teaspoon whole allspice
- ¼ teaspoon mustard seed
- 3 cups sugar
- 2 tablespoons fresh mint leaves, minced
- 1 cup white vinegar

PICKLED PEACHES

Yet another trick for canning what would otherwise spoil, this is also an alternative to pies, cobblers, and jams when the farmers markets are overflowing with cheap, luscious peaches.

In a medium saucepan, combine all ingredients except for the peaches and bring to a boil. Reduce the heat to low and cover the pot. Simmer for 5 minutes and then add the peaches to the hot liquid. Immediately remove the whole pot from the heat. Allow to cool to room temperature. Cover and chill for at least 2 hours and for up to five days.

Peaches can also be canned in a waterbath, using the same instructions as on page 155.

1 cup water

½ cup white wine vinegar

2 tablespoons sugar

2 whole cloves

1 cinnamon stick

1 tablespoon fresh ginger, grated

1 tablespoon whole mustard seed

1 pound firm, ripe peaches, peeled, pitted, and sliced ¼-inch thick

KIMCHI

Angela: My mother, Maria Koh, was born in South Korea and came to the United States about 45 years ago. She met my dad, who had escaped from North Korea as a boy with his family, while he was working at his mother's Korean restaurant.

When we were little, we never got to eat out. I mean never. Getting a pizza was a big deal, and we did that maybe twice a year—only for special occasions. But my mother was an incredible cook. There were six of us kids, and she spent all of her time sewing our clothes and cooking for a crowd.

We had an apple tree in the backyard and a garden full of everything you could think of: tomatoes, green peppers, lettuce, jalapeño peppers, squash, zucchini, carrots, peaches. You name it, my mom planted it. Due to this bountiful harvest, she would often make jams and huge batches of kimchi, which she buried in the backyard in a big garbage can-size container like they do in Korea.

She lived with Bryan and me for about five months after we moved to Asheville. And things were just like when I was a child: She cooked a lot of food for us, including big batches of the two kimchis that follow.

BAECHU
(NAPA CABBAGE)
KIMCHI

This is the type of kimchi many are accustomed to. It's a funky, spicy, cabbage-based dish that's great with a burger, on the side of ribs, or even on a barbecue sandwich for a Korean twist.

Cut Napa cabbage into quarters through the root, then slice into roughly 1-inch pieces, discarding root. Place the cabbage and daikon in a large bowl, and add the salt, rubbing it thoroughly by hand into the vegetables. Let rest for 1 to 6 hours (the more it rests, the more liquid it releases), and then rinse the cabbage and daikon in three changes of cold water. Check the vegetables to make sure they're not too salty (if they are, give them another rinse), then let them rest in a colander for 15 minutes.

Meanwhile, combine the sugar, garlic, ginger, green onions, fish sauce, and hot pepper in a small bowl. Mix the ingredients well until they form a paste, and set aside.

Squeeze any remaining water out of the cabbage and daikon, then place the vegetables into a clean bowl. Add the pepper paste and mix well. Put kimchi mixture into clean, sterilized 1-quart jars. To ferment, leave on the kitchen counter for one to five days. Check daily by opening the jars and pressing down with a clean utensil on the cabbage. Bubbling is completely normal. Refrigerate when it's the right amount of funky, which will take longer the cooler the room is.

Yield: 1 quart

- 2 pounds (about 1 head) Napa cabbage
- 1 daikon radish, peeled and cut into matchsticks (about 8 ounces)
- 2 tablespoons salt
- 2 tablespoons sugar
- 1 tablespoon minced garlic
- ½ tablespoon minced ginger
- 4 green onions, chopped
- 2 tablespoons fish sauce
- 1–3 tablespoons Korean hot pepper flakes or ½–2 teaspoons Korean ground red pepper

KKAKDUGI (RADISH) KIMCHI

Yield: 2 quarts

- 4 pounds daikon radish
- 2 tablespoons salt
- 2 tablespoons sugar
- 3 tablespoons minced garlic
- 2 tablespoons minced ginger
- 4 green onions, chopped
- 1 tablespoon fish sauce
- ½ cup of Korean red hot pepper flakes (from an Asian market)

While you might think all kimchi is cabbage-based, *Kkakdugi* is a popular type of kimchi made from diced radish. It's very common in Korea and often used in everyday meals along with the *baechu* (Napa cabbage) kimchi that is now popular in the United States.

Peel the radishes, then rinse in cold water and pat dry. Cut into ¾- to 1-inch cubes and place in a large bowl. Add salt and sugar, and mix cubes well by hand. Let stand in the bowl for about 1 hour, then drain the juice from the radish, reserving the liquid.

Add the garlic, ginger, green onions, fish sauce, hot pepper flakes, and ⅓ cup of the juice from the radish. Mix it up well by hand, until the seasonings coat all the radish cubes evenly and the radish looks juicy. Put the cubes into a glass jar and press down with clean hands or a utensil to remove any air from between the radish cubes.

Let it ferment by leaving it on the counter for a few days. When it starts fermenting, little bubbles may appear on top of the radish, and it will smell strong and sour and be ready to eat. Refrigerate when it's done fermenting.

VI rib-stickin' sides

People may initially come to 12 Bones for our ribs or our pulled pork. But what keeps them coming back again and again are the sides. People swear by the Damn Good Corn Pudding, and they're crazy about our Jalapeño Cheese Grits—and we can't say we blame them. We've honed our recipes through years of minor adjustments until they're just perfect.

HONEY CORNBREAD

What's that sweet flavor doing in our cornbread? Why that's the Yankee influence you're tasting. Southern cornbread is traditionally not sweet. Nor is it cakelike, but it improves the longer it sits out. (The better to sop up the juice from the pinto beans or black-eyed peas.)

But even many Southerners prefer a sweet, moist, cake-like cornbread these days. If you find yourself in that camp, this is going to be your go-to recipe. If you like the sweetness but want it a bit more traditional in texture, you might like this recipe best when it's a day old, when it gets a little crunchy around the edges.

Preheat the oven to 375°F. In a medium-size bowl whisk together the dry ingredients, then set them aside. In a large mixing bowl, whisk together the remaining ingredients. Add the flour mixture, then whisk it all together until incorporated, taking care not to over-mix. Spray a baking pan with pan spray. Pour the cornbread batter into the pan, and shimmy it around until it's evenly distributed. Bake for 15 minutes. Turn the pan, and bake for another 5 minutes, or until golden.

Yield: 2 dozen squares

- 2 cups all-purpose flour
- 2 cups plain cornmeal
- 1 cup sugar
- 1½ teaspoons kosher salt
- 2 tablespoons baking powder
- 2 teaspoons rubbed sage
- 1 teaspoon coarse-ground black pepper
- 1 teaspoon paprika
- ½ cup vegetable oil
- 2 eggs
- ¾ cup creamed corn
- 2 tablespoons honey
- 1 small onion, minced
- 2 cups buttermilk

CORNBREAD STUFFING

We use our house cornbread for this recipe, which, as we mentioned, is a little on the sweeter side. But otherwise, this is a fairly traditional style of cornbread stuffing.

Yield: 8–10 servings

1 tablespoon butter
1 large yellow onion, diced
1 stalk celery, diced
5 cloves garlic
8 ounces raw breakfast sausage
   (or 12 Bones House Sausage, page 47)
1 tablespoon kosher salt
1 teaspoon sage
1 teaspoon poultry seasoning

1 teaspoon black pepper
1 teaspoon Old Bay seasoning
½ teaspoon dried oregano
½ teaspoon dried thyme
4 cups 12 Bones Pork Stock (page 59)
   or chicken stock
4 eggs
1½ pounds cornbread, crumbled

Preheat the oven to 300°F. Melt the butter in a large frying pan. Sweat the onion, celery, and garlic for 2 minutes. Add the sausage and brown over medium heat. While the meat is cooking, stir together the remaining ingredients, minus the cornbread, in a large mixing bowl. Add the cornbread and the meat mixture to the bowl and combine. Pour the stuffing into a greased 9 x 11-inch casserole dish, and then bake for 1 to 1½ hours, or until the center is set.

CHEDDAR-JALAPEÑO
SKILLET CORNBREAD

Serves 8–10

- ½ cup vegetable oil, plus 2 tablespoons
- 1½ cup plain cornmeal, plus ¼ cup
- 1 tablespoon baking powder
- 1 teaspoon kosher salt
- 3 tablespoons sugar
- 4 eggs
- 1 cup sour cream
- 1 cup creamed corn
- 1 cup extra sharp cheddar, grated
- 1 onion, diced
- 4 jalapeños, seeded and diced small

This is a truer Southern cornbread than our house cornbread, which means it's not as sweet as what we serve daily. It has a very mild heat, which the cheddar cheese tempers.

Preheat oven to 425°F. Pour 2 tablespoons of oil into a 10-inch cast iron skillet or a 10-inch cake pan. Smear the oil on the bottom and edges of the pan with a paper towel. Dust the entire pan with ¼ cup of cornmeal, discarding any excess.

In a small mixing bowl, whisk together 1½ cups cornmeal with the baking powder, salt, and sugar, and set aside.

In a medium mixing bowl, whisk together the remaining ingredients. With a spatula, fold the dry mixture into the wet mixture until everything is thoroughly combined.

Pour the batter into the greased pan and bake for 15 minutes. Lower the oven temperature to 350°F, and bake for 20 minutes, or until the top is golden brown and a toothpick inserted into the middle comes out clean. Let the cornbread cool at room temperature for 30 minutes before slicing.

DAMN GOOD CORN PUDDING

This is exactly what it sounds like—damn good corn pudding. The recipe came about when we were trying to make corn pancakes in our early days. As a testament to just how naïve we were, we thought we could make those pancakes to order, you know, since we weren't expecting to be all that busy. That lasted about a week.

We had to figure out a way to serve something like that dish, but quicker, and the idea of the corn pudding was born. These days we make this by the truckload, and we still sell out of it. But thanks to the unfussy nature of the dish—especially compared to pancakes—this recipe is great for a group or a frazzled host. You can even serve it straight out of the casserole dish.

Preheat the oven to 300°F. Mix all the dry ingredients together in a medium-size bowl. Pour the eggs, butter, cream, and creamed corn into a large mixing bowl, and beat with an electric mixer or stir until thoroughly combined. Add the poblanos and corn. Slowly add the flour mixture, and mix until just combined. The mixture should resemble cake batter. Grease a large 11 x 15-inch rimmed baking dish. Pour the pudding mixture into the pan, and place it in the oven. Lightly tent the pan with foil. Bake for 1 hour with the foil on, then remove the foil and bake for an additional 30 minutes, or until the center is just set.

Yield: 8–10 servings

- 1 ¾ cups all-purpose flour
- 1 ¼ cups sugar
- 3 tablespoons baking powder, plus 1 teaspoon
- 2 teaspoons salt
- ½ teaspoon red pepper flakes
- 1 teaspoon cumin
- 1 teaspoon coriander
- 6 large eggs
- 1 stick melted butter
- 2 cups heavy cream
- 1 14-ounce can of creamed corn
- 2 fresh poblano peppers, seeded and diced
- 1 ½ cups fresh or frozen corn kernels

JALAPEÑO CHEESE GRITS

Yield: 4–6 servings

2 cups milk

1½ cups water

2 ounces butter

1 cup stone-ground grits

1½ teaspoons kosher salt

1 teaspoon chopped jalapeño

1 teaspoon chopped red bell pepper

1 tablespoon chopped poblano pepper

2 ounces grated yellow cheddar cheese

2 ounces grated pepper Jack cheese

This side is a 12 Bones original, since Southerners think of grits as a breakfast dish—and most Northerners don't think of grits at all. To dress it up more as a side appropriate for lunch (or dinner), we've added sharp cheese and peppers. The key to a great batch is to make sure to use stone-ground grits. They might be harder to find, but they're worth the effort. In a pinch, you can use white polenta, but it has to be coarse enough to bloom and have some texture to it. The coarse-ground grits are easy to order online if you want the real deal.

Combine the milk, water, and butter in a heavy-bottomed saucepan, and heat on medium while stirring until the butter has melted. Stir in the grits, then reduce the heat to low. Simmer the grits, stirring occasionally, until they have absorbed most of the liquid and begun to thicken, otherwise referred to as "bloom." Stir in the salt and the remaining ingredients, and remove the grits from the heat. Continue to stir the grits until the cheese has fully melted.

ingredient spotlight:
POBLANOS

With the shifting cultural landscape and the general public's increasing tolerance for spice, hot peppers are more readily available than ever. It's increasingly common to find several varieties of chilies in the most basic of grocery stores, from jalapeños to habaneros.

We use poblanos, which can be found in most Mexican markets and well-stocked grocery stores, in many of our recipes. We like the pepper's mild chili flavor and its versatility. When roasted, green poblanos take on a smoky flavor and are excellent chopped and added to corn relish or blended with stock, aromatics, and cream to make a green-chili bisque. Though they're best known for their integral role in a chili relleno, at 12 Bones, we use them in our corn pudding to help temper the sweetness a bit.

Ripe poblanos turn a reddish-brown color and are both sweeter and spicier than the green peppers. Dried, poblanos become ancho peppers and are a staple of Mexican cooking. We blend dried ancho chilies into a paste, which we use to season some of our barbecue sauces with a smoky, lingering heat. See page 66 for the recipe.

BLACK-EYED PEAS
WITH JALAPEÑOS

Yield: 6–8 servings

- 1 pound raw breakfast sausage (or 12 Bones House Sausage, page 47)
- 1 yellow onion, diced
- 5 cloves garlic, rough chopped
- 1 tablespoon salt
- 1 tablespoon ground cumin
- 1 tablespoon ground sage
- 6 cups 12 Bones Pork Stock (page 59) or chicken stock
- 2-pound bag frozen black-eyed peas
- 4 jalapeños, diced (remove stems and seeds)

The black-eyed pea likely originated in Africa. Also known as cowpeas, they're often eaten in the American South as a good-luck charm for wealth in the New Year. Some say that's because the little legumes look like coins. But Southern lore has it that black-eyed peas were once considered animal fodder by Northerners. During General William T. Sherman's march to the sea during the Civil War, Northern troops attempted to destroy the Southerners' crops in an attempt to leave them high and dry.

But they didn't waste any time setting fire to the peas, since they weren't considered food by the Yankees. And the Northerners had already made off with most of the cattle that would have subsisted on the peas. Those little peas helped many a Southerner through the winter and have been symbolic of a fresh start ever since.

At 12 Bones, this is one of the few recipes where we choose frozen over fresh. We find frozen black-eyed peas hold up better to cooking than dried beans; they won't go mushy. This dish, served steaming hot on a cold day, goes great with Cheddar-Jalapeño Skillet Cornbread (page 169).

In a 4- to 6-quart pot, brown the sausage with the onions and garlic. Strain off the fat. Return the sausage mixture to the pot, then add the seasonings. Cook while stirring over medium heat until the spices are fragrant, about 3 minutes. Add the remaining ingredients, and continue to cook until the liquid has reduced and is level with peas. Taste and adjust seasoning.

SMOKY BAKED BEANS

When we first opened, what's now called the River Arts District was mostly full of warehouses and working-class gentlemen. One group of guys who became regulars worked at the Riverside Stump Dump, a business that makes mulch out of scrap wood. (It looks like a big pile of wood chips by the road.) The Stump Dump guys were just crazy about beans, and they'd call us every day and ask for them. We'd tell them we had white beans, black beans, whatever beans we had on at the time, but we never had the right beans, according to the Stump guys. We quickly learned that in North Carolina, "beans" means "baked beans," particularly when they're coming with 'cue.

Eventually, we started working on an idea, something for the people who wanted baked beans. We're not sure how long it took us, but it wasn't as fast as some would have preferred. Still, we were dead set on the notion that baked beans weren't going to be our specialty. That was until Broadus Brannon, a former Kansas City Barbecue Society judge, walked in the door.

"He was the one who introduced us to the idea of smoking the beans," says 12 Bones founder Tom. "You would think that we would have figured that out." The smoked baked beans, of course, were a huge hit.

Yield: 4–6 servings
2 ounces diced bacon
1 small carrot, grated
1 small onion, diced small
⅔ cup ketchup
⅓ cup dark brown sugar
¾ teaspoon kosher salt
½ cup 12 Bones Tomato "Q" Sauce (page 102)
½ cup 12 Bones Tangy Mustard "Q" sauce (page 115)
¼ cup of water
1 bay leaf
6 cups cooked or canned navy beans, rinsed and drained

In a 4- to 6-quart saucepan, cook the bacon over medium heat until the fat is rendered and the bacon is crispy, stirring with a wooden spoon to allow the bacon to cook evenly. Reduce the heat to low, and stir in the grated carrot and the onion, cooking until the onion has softened. Remove the bacon mixture from the heat, then stir in the ketchup, sugar, salt, sauces, and water, then add the bay leaf. Return the pan to medium heat, and stir the mixture to dissolve the sugar. Transfer the sauce to a 9 x 13-inch casserole dish. Fold in the beans carefully so that you don't crush them. Chill for a least 1 hour or overnight to allow the beans to soak up the flavor.

Just before serving, smoke the beans uncovered in the casserole dish over indirect heat at 250 to 275°F, or until hot. (See page 13 for more on smoking.)

MUSHROOM AND SAUSAGE CASSEROLE

Yield: 8 servings

For the cheese sauce:

⅓ cup milk

¼ cup heavy cream

½ teaspoon Worcestershire sauce

¼ teaspoon hot sauce

⅛ teaspoon kosher salt

4 ounces white American cheese

2 ounces white cheddar, grated

For the casserole:

1 pound whole button mushrooms, cleaned

8 ounces raw breakfast sausage, or your choice of homemade sausage (page 42)

1 small yellow onion, diced

1 red bell pepper, diced

4 cloves garlic, chopped

1 cup cheese sauce

8 ounces of cornbread, crumbled (or substitute store-bought bread crumbs)

1 teaspoon kosher salt

1 teaspoon ground ginger

1 teaspoon ground sage

1 teaspoon ground cumin

1 cup grated Parmesan

This recipe used to be vegetarian. But then one year, the price of mushrooms went through the roof. Our sausage, which we make with trim from our high-quality meat, is practically free. So we replaced half of the mushrooms with sausage, ending up with something that was more cost-effective for us and, ultimately, more flavorful. Sorry, vegetarians.

We still make it to this day, but usually with a 2:1 ratio of mushrooms to sausage. It's a great way to use leftover cornbread, in keeping with the Southern tradition of using absolutely everything.

To make the cheese sauce, add the milk, cream, Worcestershire, hot sauce, and salt to a medium, heavy-bottomed saucepan and stir with a wooden spoon. Simmer on medium-low heat, just until you see steam. Add the cheeses to the mixture and stir constantly until the cheese melts with no lumps.

To make the casserole, preheat the oven to 400°F. Place the mushrooms in one layer on a baking tray. Roast the mushrooms, uncovered, in the oven for 15 minutes. Remove the mushrooms from the oven, and, set aside to cool. Reduce the oven heat to 350°F. Brown the sausage in a skillet with the onion, red bell pepper, and garlic. Transfer this mixture to a large mixing bowl with the mushrooms and the remaining ingredients, except for the Parmesan. Mix well, then transfer to a greased casserole dish. Top with Parmesan and bake in the oven until the top is golden brown, about 40 minutes.

MACARONI AND CHEESE

This is a somewhat simple version of a classic American comfort food dish. OK, it's not as quick as boxed mac-and-cheese, of course, but you'll find it's far better. This is a huge hit as a hearty side at the restaurant, maybe because it's the ideal substitution for anyone who's not a corn pudding fan.

Preheat oven to 375°F. Grease a 3-quart casserole dish, then add the cooked pasta to the casserole dish. Set aside.

To make the cheese sauce, add the milk, cream, Worcestershire, hot sauce, and salt to a medium, heavy-bottomed saucepan and stir with a wooden spoon. Simmer on medium-low heat, just until you see steam. Add the cheeses to the milk sauce, and stir constantly until the cheese melts and the sauce is smooth.

For the Macaroni and Cheese:
Our ratio is 1 cup of cheese sauce per 1 quart of cooked elbow macaroni, though you may choose to use a higher cheese-to-pasta ratio. For best results, mix half of the cheese sauce with the pasta, then add the rest of the cheese sauce.

Pour the cheese sauce over the top and mix gently. If using, add an even layer of grated cheese over the top, then finish with the bread crumbs. Bake uncovered for about 30 minutes, or until the sauce is bubbling and the top is golden brown.

Yield: 4–6 servings

For the Macaroni and cheese

- 6 cups dried elbow pasta, cooked
- 3 cups cheese sauce (recipe follows)
- 6 ounces grated cheddar (optional)
- 1 cup bread crumbs (optional)

For the cheese sauce:

- 1 cup whole milk
- ½ cup heavy cream
- 1½ teaspoon Worcestershire sauce
- 1 teaspoon hot sauce
- ½ teaspoon salt
- 10 ounces white American cheese, diced small
- 2 ounces grated white cheddar

WARM GERMAN POTATO SALAD

Yield: 8 servings

- 5 pounds nonwaxy potatoes, such as Yukon Golds or Russets, skin on, diced into ½-inch cubes or small wedges
- ⅓ cup vegetable oil
- 2 tablespoons Old Bay seasoning
- 2 teaspoons ground black pepper
- 1 teaspoon celery seeds
- 2 tablespoons kosher salt
- 1 teaspoon red pepper flakes
- 1 teaspoon sugar
- 4 ounces of butter, melted
- 2 large yellow onions, julienned
- ½ cup white vinegar
- ¼ cup spicy brown mustard

We love this salad as an alternative to the traditionally mayonnaise-choked dish that you often find on the table at Southern potlucks and Sunday suppers. (Not that there's anything wrong with that, of course.) It's good cold, too, which makes it a tasty side for a summer picnic.

Preheat the oven to 400°F. Toss the potatoes with the oil, seasonings, sugar, butter, and yellow onions. Transfer the potato mixture to a shallow baking pan, large enough for it all to fit in one layer. Roast, uncovered, for 15 minutes.

Remove the pan from the oven. Scrape the potatoes loose from the bottom of pan with a spatula and flip. Return the potatoes to the oven, and roast until they're tender. Remove from the oven, and place in a large mixing bowl. Toss with the vinegar and mustard. Taste and adjust seasoning, if necessary. Serve warm.

SMOKED POTATO SALAD

What's better than potato salad? Smoked potato salad, of course. This is a beautiful dish for vegetarians in a meat-eating household, since the potatoes pick up plenty of luscious smoke flavor without actually touching any meat. The cilantro-spiked dressing that goes on these potatoes helps to cut through, and ends up complementing, the smoke. This also makes a great cookout side with grilled corn on the cob.

Simmer potatoes until they are softened but still slightly firm (when stuck with a paring knife, they should not slip off, but not feel raw). Drain well and toss with the vegetable oil, salt, black pepper, and chili powder. Smoke at 250 to 275°F for 40 to 45 minutes, or until tender and fully cooked. Meanwhile, whisk together the dressing ingredients in a medium bowl. Crush the potatoes and cool. Once the potatoes have cooled to room temperature, fold in three-quarters of the dressing. Check the consistency and continue to add dressing as needed.

Yield: 10–12 servings, 1 cup each

For the potatoes:

- 5 pounds new red potatoes, peeled and halved
- 2 tablespoons vegetable oil
- 2 teaspoons salt
- 1 teaspoon black pepper
- 1 teaspoon chili powder

For the dressing:

- 1 onion, minced
- 2 stalks celery, small diced
- 1 bunch cilantro, chopped
- 10 cloves garlic, minced
- 3 cups mayonnaise
- ½ cup Gulden's spicy brown mustard
- 2 tablespoons dark brown sugar
- 1 teaspoon celery salt
- 1 teaspoon red pepper flakes
- 1 cup cider vinegar

WHITE CHEDDAR
SPUDS

Yield: 10 servings

- 5 pounds Idaho potatoes
- 1 cup heavy cream
- 1 cup whole milk
- 1 stick of butter
- 1 tablespoon salt
- 1 teaspoon black pepper
- 8 ounces white American cheese (diced small)
- 8 ounces white cheddar, grated

Chef Shane likes to jokingly call these "high-end mashed potatoes." The rest of us just call them delicious. With all the cheese and the starch in the potatoes, you have to be careful when you're mixing this dish up. If you stir the potatoes too much, you might as well use this for wall spackle rather than a side dish.

Clean the potatoes and cut out any rough spots or eyes. Place the potatoes in a large pot and cover them with water. Bring the water to a boil, and then reduce the heat to low. Simmer until the potatoes are tender, but not splitting open.

While the potatoes are cooking, heat the cream, milk, and butter on low until the butter is fully melted. Next, add the salt, pepper, and American cheese. Continue to cook on low while stirring constantly, until the cheese has melted. Remove the cheese mixture from the heat, then stir in the cheddar.

Once the potatoes are done, strain them thoroughly and mash in a large mixing bowl. Then gently fold in the cheese sauce.

Variations:

For Pepper Jack Spuds, replace the cheddar with 10 ounces of pepper jack, diced small.

For Horseradish Spuds, replace both cheeses with 6 tablespoons of prepared horseradish, and add 1 extra teaspoon of salt.

For Roasted Garlic Spuds, replace cheeses with ½ cup of 12 Bones Roasted Garlic (page 55), mash with spuds, and add 1 extra teaspoon of salt.

SMOKED GOUDA
DROP BISCUITS

We came up with this recipe when we found a great source for Gouda from the local farmers' market. These savory biscuits are easy to make and turn out crunchy on the outside, creamy on the inside. There's a touch of smokiness at the very end, which you can cut by using cheese that isn't smoked. We serve these with pinto beans for a hearty lunch special.

Preheat the oven to 400°F. Line a cookie sheet with parchment paper or a silicone baking mat. In a medium mixing bowl, whisk together the flour, baking powder, baking soda, salt, sugar, cheese, oregano, and pepper.

Next, stir in the butter. Empty the contents of the bowl onto a clean, dry work surface. Mound the dough together, and begin to smear "down the mountain" with the palm of your hand. Continue this process until all the butter pieces are smeared.

Return the dough to the bowl. Make a well in the center of the dough, and pour the buttermilk in the center of the well. Using your hands, fold the dough into the buttermilk until well combined. The dough will be very moist, so don't be concerned.

Using two tablespoons, drop golf ball-size dough balls onto the lined cookie sheet, leaving a 2-inch space between the biscuits. Bake the biscuits for about 15 minutes, or until the edges begin to crisp.

Yield: About 20 biscuits

- 2 cups all-purpose flour
- 1 tablespoon baking powder
- ¼ teaspoon baking soda
- ½ teaspoon kosher salt
- 2 tablespoons sugar
- 1 cup smoked Gouda cheese, grated
- 1 tablespoon fresh oregano, chopped
- 1 teaspoon coarse-ground black pepper
- 4 ounces butter, cold, cut into ½-inch pieces
- 1 cup whole buttermilk, cold

MASHED SWEET POTATOES

Yields: 6 servings

4 large sweet potatoes, peeled and halved

¼ cup heavy cream

½ stick salted butter

3 tablespoons dark brown sugar

1½ teaspoon salt

1 teaspoon chili powder

½ cup grated Parmesan cheese

Sweet potatoes are not actually potatoes, but rather a starchy member of the morning glory family. And the sweet, orange-fleshed tubers that we love to consume on Thanksgiving are not, in fact, yams. Whatever they are, we tend to love our sweet potatoes, candied and swimming in viscous syrup or mashed with pumpkin pie spices and butter.

But this recipe is neither candied nor holiday-themed. Though we do add sugar and plenty of butter (not to mention cheese and cream) to this recipe, we forego the winter spice route and use chili powder instead. We think you'll find the use of chili powder cuts down on the sometimes cloying flavor of mashed sweet potatoes, taking them into more of a savory realm. Try serving this dish on the side of roasted pork or with a big mess of ribs rather than on your Thanksgiving table.

Cover the potatoes with water in a medium pot. Bring the water to a boil on high, and then reduce the heat to low. Simmer the sweet potatoes until they are tender but not mushy. Test the doneness with a knife or fork. Combine the cream and butter in a saucepan or large skillet and cook at a simmer. Scrape the bottom occasionally with a wooden spoon to prevent scorching. Once the butter is fully melted, remove the cream mixture from the heat and then stir in the sugar, salt, and chili powder. Set aside. Strain the potatoes, reserving 1 cup of the liquid. Mash the hot potatoes with the Parmesan in a large bowl. Next, add the wet mixture and fold it gently into the potatoes until incorporated. If the potatoes are too dry, add some of reserved liquid. Do not overmix, or the potatoes will become too starchy.

BRUNSWICK
STEW

Brunswick stew may have originated as a squirrel-based dish, but these days the meat is culled more often from the grocery store shelves. Before we had it on the menu, people asked why we didn't all the time. It's often a smokehouse standard as it's a great repository for brisket ends, which don't look so nice on the plate but work just fine chopped and in a stew.

This particular recipe also uses chicken legs. We're pretty firm on chicken legs instead of breast, in case you're wondering whether you can make any substitutions. The reason being that in this recipe white meat can become so stringy you can practically floss your teeth with it.

Heat the oil in a heavy-bottomed 3- to 4-quart saucepan over medium-high heat until it begins to shimmer. Add onion, and reduce the heat to medium-low. Stir constantly. Once the onion is soft, add the garlic and continue to stir for 2 minutes. Next, add the canned tomatoes and the stock. Add the smoked salt while stirring, and raise heat to medium-high until the stew boils.

Reduce the heat to medium and stir in the remaining ingredients, one at a time. Once all the ingredients are incorporated, reduce the heat to low and simmer, uncovered, for 30 minutes. Stir occasionally. Remove from heat and adjust seasonings to taste.

Yield: About 4 servings

- 3 tablespoons vegetable oil
- 1 yellow onion, peeled and medium diced
- 5 cloves 12 Bones Roasted Garlic, rough chopped (page 55), or substitute regular garlic
- 2 14.5-ounce cans of fire-roasted diced tomatoes with juice
- 2 cups chicken or beef stock
- 2 tablespoons smoked sea salt
- 1 teaspoon Old Bay Seasoning
- 1 teaspoon ground black pepper
- 4 ounces of smoked beef brisket, chopped
- 2 smoked chicken legs, meat pulled and chopped (optional)
- ½ cup fresh or frozen lima beans
- ½ cup creamed corn
- ½ cup 12 Bones Tomato "Q" Sauce (page 104) or any sweet, mild tomato barbecue sauce
- 1 tablespoon hot sauce (optional)

VII southern treats and homemade sweets

At 12 Bones, we've got your number on the sweet front. It may have all started with the humble chocolate chip cookie and a borrowed pecan pie recipe, but over the years we've slowly added to our dessert repertoire— ask any of our regulars. Those in the know like to ask what Chef Shane has up his sleeve. Sometimes it's simple stuff, like Granny's Apple Crisp. But sometimes, Shane's in the back with sawed-off PVC pipes, molding gorgeous stacked cakes like the Tres Leches Strawberry Shortcake on page 213. It's to die for, but don't worry about the DIY dessert mold approach. That's optional.

PECAN PIE

Early on at 12 Bones, Brad Daugherty, of NASCAR, NBA, and UNC basketball fame, came in and noticed our pie selection was a bit lackluster. He recommended we let his mother-in-law, Betty, make some pies for us. We gave her a ring and found that she was a true Southern mom through and through: funny, loud, and forthcoming. Betty brought some pies by and, sure enough, they were outrageously good. What was the secret? "All I know is there's lots of sugar and salt, so they've gotta be good," said Brad Daugherty. However, once we were serving hundreds of slices per week, Betty (understandably) grew tired of making pies. So she gave us her recipes to carry on the tradition.

Preheat the oven to 350°F. Use a 10-inch pie plate.

If using a scratch crust: On a slightly floured work surface, roll out one disk of dough to ⅛-inch thickness. Lightly dust the top with flour, roll back onto rolling pin, and drape into a greased pie pan. Then, flute the edges. Cover with parchment paper, add some pie weights, and bake in the center of the oven for 15 minutes, or until edges start to brown. Carefully remove parchment with pie weights and return to oven for another 10 minutes. Cool on a wire rack for at least 15 minutes or up to an hour.

Or skip these steps and use a frozen crust and follow the instructions on the package.

To make the filling, combine the eggs, cream, vanilla, and salt in a large mixing bowl and whisk. Set aside.

Then, melt the butter in a small saucepan over low heat. Once it is fully melted, first add the corn syrup to the butter, and then whisk in the dark brown sugar, stirring until it is smooth. Increase the heat to medium, and bring to a slow simmer, until the perimeter of the mixture starts to bubble ever so slightly in the pot.

Remove the pot from the heat and slowly, while whisking, drizzle the hot syrup into the egg mixture until fully incorporated. If you try to rush this step, you might end up with scrambled eggs. Once the syrup is thoroughly combined, add pecan pieces to pie shell and immediately fill with syrup right up to the fluted edges.

Bake the pie at 350°F for 25 minutes, then spin the pie a half-turn and bake for another 10 minutes. Once the pie is done, remove it from the oven to cool. As soon as it comes out of the oven, tap the middle of the pie lightly with a fork to flatten and decompress the center. Your pie will crater if this is not done.

Yield: 6–8 slices

- ½ recipe pie dough (page 215)
- 3 eggs
- ½ cup heavy cream
- ¾ teaspoon vanilla
- ¼ teaspoon salt
- 3 tablespoons butter
- ¾ cup light corn syrup
- 5 ounces dark brown sugar
- 1 cup pecans

KEY LIME PIE

This came about when we needed a dessert with a little twang. And Key Lime Pie is a favorite, no matter where you are when the temperature rises. When making this pie, stick to the recipe—don't try to put too much of your own spin to it. If you add too much butter, the crust will creep down the sides when you bake it. If you bake it at too high a temperature, it will crack. It's like any custard; you have to be careful with it.

First, preheat the oven to 375°F.

For the crust, melt the butter over low heat in a small sauce pan. Then combine all of the ingredients in a large mixing bowl and mix thoroughly. Chill in the refrigerator for at least 20 minutes. If you're going to leave this overnight, you'll have to wrap it.

Combine all the filling ingredients into a mixing bowl and use a whisk to blend until smooth. Tap the bowl on the counter to try to release any air bubbles.

Lightly grease a 10-inch pie pan with pan spray or butter. Press the crust into the pan, so that the edges are flush with the pie pan and firmly packed into place. Bake your prepared shell at 375°F for 10 minutes or until the edges turn light brown. Next, allow the shell to cool. Lower the oven's heat to 350°F.

Once the shell is cooled, fill it with the Key lime filling. Create a shallow water bath in a deep sheet pan, and place the pie pan in the water bath, making sure not to get any water on the pie. Bake for 20 minutes, then turn the pie a half turn. Continue baking until the filling is set, about another 10 minutes. Let the pie cool to room temperature before refrigerating.

Chill for at least 1 hour before slicing. We slice our pies into eighths. If not serving the pie right away, cover it with plastic wrap and return to the fridge. The pie will keep for up to five days.

Yield: 6–8 slices

For the crust:

1 cup graham cracker crumbs

¼ cup white sugar

3 ounces butter

¼ cup toasted and finely ground pecans

3 tablespoons shredded toasted coconut

⅛ teaspoon cinnamon

¼ teaspoon salt

For the filling:

1 ¾ cups sweetened condensed milk

4 egg yolks

⅓ cup Key lime juice

2 tablespoons sugar

Kent on:
KEY LIME

Though many may (and do) question how anyone eating at 12 Bones could possibly leave room for dessert, Kent Wolff, a loan officer for Mountain Lifestyles Mortgage in Asheville, isn't one to pass up the pie.

"There are those of us who appreciate it so sufficiently much that we put the rest of our meal in a to-go container in anticipation of that Key lime pie," he said.

To Wolff, 12 Bones' Key lime pie is reminiscent of the one his great aunt Betty made. Betty lived in Fort Pierce, Florida, and often picked her own Key limes. "I was always fond of her recipe, and 12 Bones' recipe patterns hers most similarly," said Wolff.

Though 12 Bones' dessert menu is wide and varied, you could certainly fool Wolff into thinking it contains only that Key lime pie. "I'm not convinced 12 Bones has another dessert as far as I'm concerned—besides PBR," he said.

CHOCOLATE CHIP COOKIES

You know what you're getting here: good, classic, chocolate chip cookies. We keep these right by the register, on a plate, prewrapped and ready to go. Lots of people carry these out of the restaurant with them—for some reason, it seems like they just don't have room for dessert right away.

In cookie law, it's usually forbidden to overmix flour, because you don't want to work too much gluten into the batter—but in this recipe, you do. It helps to give the cookies enough structure so that they don't spread out too much in the oven.

Preheat oven to 375°F. In a stand-up mixer fitted with a paddle attachment, beat the butter and margarine with the sugars until the mixture is light in color and fluffy. Scrape down the sides of bowl. While the butter mixture is creaming, whisk together flour, baking soda, and salt in a separate bowl. Once the butter mixture is fluffy and no longer grainy, mix in one egg at a time followed by the vanilla. Add the flour mixture, and pulse until most of the dry ingredients are moist.

Yield: About 20 cookies
8 ounces butter, softened
8 ounces margarine, softened
1½ cups sugar
1 cup dark brown sugar
4 cups all-purpose flour
2 teaspoons baking soda
1 teaspoon kosher salt
4 eggs
2 teaspoons vanilla extract
3 cups semisweet or milk chocolate chips

Remove the bowl and scrape down the sides until no more white flour is visible. Return the bowl to the mixer, and beat on medium for 10 seconds. This will help form a little gluten to give the cookies some backbone while baking.

Scoop the dough onto a cookie pan lined with parchment paper or a silicone mat, using a 2-ounce ice-cream scoop, keeping the scoops about 2 inches apart. Chill pan until dough has hardened. Bake cookies about 12 minutes, turning the pan halfway through.

Cooking time will vary depending on the size of your cookie balls. Excess dough can be sealed tightly and frozen or stored in a refrigerator for up to a week.

Note: We tried to make a batch of these cookies with a hand mixer to see if it would work, but unfortunately the experiment failed miserably. The dough was grainy, the cookies spread too much while baking, and the poor hand mixer almost caught on fire.

GINGER STOUT SNAPS

Yield: About 28 cookies

For the stout syrup:

2 quarts stout beer

1 cup sugar

For the cookies:

2 cups all-purpose flour

2 teaspoons baking soda

2 teaspoons ground ginger

1 teaspoon ground
   cinnamon

½ teaspoon ground allspice

½ teaspoon ground cloves

¼ teaspoon of kosher salt

4 ounces melted butter

½ cup stout syrup

¼ cup molasses

½ cup sugar

½ cup packed dark
   brown sugar

1 large egg

4 ounces candied ginger,
   rough chopped (page
   201, or use store bought,
   though it's not as good)

½ cup crystallized ginger
   sugar or turbinado sugar

Black Mocha Stout is a beer made by the Highland Brewing Company, which opened in Asheville in 1994, kicking off the craft beer revolution in Western North Carolina. Maybe it was the beer's influence, but Shane got distracted and accidentally mixed the wet ingredients together for a ginger snap recipe and a stout brownie recipe he was working on.

If you don't have access to Highland's beers, it's perfectly fine to substitute another chocolaty stout.

To make the stout syrup, in a 4- to 6-quart heavy-bottom saucepan, stir together the beer and sugar over medium heat, until the sugar has dissolved. Once the sugar is dissolved, stop stirring and increase the heat to medium-high. Boil the beer syrup until it is reduced to about 2 cups. This should take about 30 minutes. When ready, syrup should resemble molasses and should coat the back of a spoon.

Line a cookie sheet with parchment paper or a silicone mat and preheat the oven to 375°F. In a medium bowl, whisk together the flour, baking soda, ground ginger, cinnamon, allspice, cloves, and salt and set aside. In a large mixing bowl, whisk together the butter, stout syrup, molasses, sugar, brown sugar, and egg. Stir in the flour mixture and the candied ginger until the batter is thoroughly combined.

Roll the cookie dough in between the palms of your hands to form golf ball-size rounds. Roll the balls in the ginger sugar, then place them on the lined cookie sheet, leaving 2 inches distance between the cookies to allow them to spread out while they cook. Chill for 10 minutes.

Using a small piece of wax or parchment paper, slightly mash down on each ball and then bake for 12 to 15 minutes, or until the cookies have spread out and the edges are beginning to crisp. Remove the cookies from the oven, and cool on a wire rack before serving.

CANDIED GINGER

Yield: About 2 cups

1   pound fresh ginger
    (preferably Hawaiian,
    peeled and sliced ⅛ inch
    thick, across the grain)

5   cups water

1   pound sugar
    (approximately)

Use these ginger pieces in the Ginger Stout Snaps, on ice cream, or just eat 'em plain. We have it on good authority that candied ginger is good for a hangover as well.

Spray a cooking rack lightly with pan spray. Set the rack in a half sheet pan, lined with a silicone mat or parchment paper. Place the ginger and water in a 2- to 4-quart saucepan. Cook over medium heat until the ginger is tender, about 30 to 40 minutes. Drain the ginger in a colander or sieve, reserving ¼ cup of the liquid. Weigh the ginger after thoroughly draining. Then weigh out an equal amount of sugar. Add the ginger and the reserved liquid back to the pan. Stir in the sugar. Cook over medium-high heat, and bring to a boil while stirring. Reduce the heat to medium, and stir frequently until the mixture becomes dry, about 20 minutes.

Immediately remove the ginger from the heat, and spread it in an even layer over the wire rack, taking care to make sure that the pieces are not touching. Allow the ginger to cool to room temperature. Store the pieces in an airtight container, and store the crystallized sugar in a separate airtight container.

BLUEBERRY
OATMEAL COOKIES

This recipe started out as a regular old oatmeal cookie recipe. But one morning, Chef Shane's wife stirred blueberries into her oatmeal, and the scent of oats and berries drifted through the kitchen, inspiring him to go a different route. It was an instant classic. Now, the blueberry cookies far outsell the original recipe with raisins. We just can't keep these in the house.

> **Note:** If using cardamom pods, remove the seeds from the pod by giving them a firm whack using a knife laid flat or a rolling pin. Toast the seeds in a small sauté pan until they're nice and fragrant. Make sure to keep them moving constantly in the pan while toasting to prevent them from burning. Remove the seeds from the heat, then dump them on a clean plate to cool for a bit. Crush the seeds with a rolling pin or in a mortar and pestle. Or skip these steps and use ground cardamom.

Toss the oats with the blueberry-pomegranate juice in a small mixing bowl, and set that aside. In a separate bowl, whisk together the flour, baking soda, cinnamon, nutmeg, and cardamom, then set aside. Next, melt the butter in a medium-size saucepan. Remove the butter from the heat and whisk into it the two types of sugar and the salt. Transfer that mixture to a large mixing bowl, and whisk into it the the egg, vanilla, and zest, then fold in the flour mixture. Fold in the oats mixture and the dried blueberries, then wrap the bowl with plastic wrap and chill overnight, or at least 2 hours, to soften the oats.

Preheat your oven to 375°F. While you wait for it to warm up, line a cookie sheet with a silicone mat or parchment paper. Put on gloves if you'd prefer to not get your hands sticky, and roll the cookie batter into golf ball-size pieces between the palms of your hands. Place the cookie balls on the prepared cookie sheet, leaving 2 inches between each ball. Flatten the cookies ever so slightly with the palm of your hand. Bake for 15 to 20 minutes, turning the cookies about halfway through the process. You'll know that the cookies are done when the edges turn golden brown and the centers are set.

Remove the cookies from the oven and allow them to cool for about 20 minutes before you serve them. Leftover cookies can be stored in an airtight container for up to five days at room temperature.

Yield: About 1 dozen cookies

- 2 cups old-fashioned rolled oats
- ¼ cup pomegranate-blueberry juice
- 1¼ cup all-purpose flour
- ½ teaspoon baking soda
- 1 teaspoon ground cinnamon
- ¼ teaspoon fresh grated nutmeg
- 4 cardamom pods (or 1 teaspoon of ground cardamom)
- 8 ounces butter
- ½ cup light brown sugar
- ½ cup sugar
- ½ teaspoon kosher salt
- 1 egg
- 1 teaspoon vanilla
- Zest from one lemon, preferably organic and unwaxed
- 2 cups dried blueberries, preferably wild (you will need to get extra to nibble on)

GRANNY'S APPLE CRISP

We pride ourselves on the small tweaks, some would say improvements, we make to classic recipes. It took us many, many experiments, trying to develop something a step up from the typical apple crisp, but we eventually got there.

Granny Smith apples are tart and acidic, but we found coconut milk perfectly tempered the fruit's bite. Our other trick is cutting the apples, tossing them with our seasonings, and letting them sit overnight before we bake them. The apples release a liquid that's rich with sugar, spices, and apple essence, which can then be reduced and folded back in with the fruit.

This recipe handles adjustments well. You can substitute some dried fruit soaked in liqueur to the apples, you can add other fruits to it, and you can even toss in some candied ginger (page 201). Anything that goes with apples will do.

To make the crumb topping, whisk together the brown sugar and flour. Dump the butter cubes in all at once, and mix it together with your hands until it resembles coarse cornmeal. You can use the topping right away or store the mixture in the freezer until you're ready to use it. Just transfer it to freezer bags right after you make it, and try to squeeze out any air to avoid freezer burn. Toss it in the freezer and store for up to three months.

To assemble the crisp, in a medium mixing bowl, toss the apples with the brown sugar, salt, and all the spices. Cover the seasoned apples, and refrigerate them overnight or for at least 4 hours.

Yield: 6 servings

For the crumb topping:

- 5 cups packed dark brown sugar
- 5 cups all-purpose flour
- ½ pound butter, cold, cut into 24 cubes

For the apples:

- 3 pounds Granny Smith apples, peeled, cored, and cut into ¼-inch wedges
- 2 cups packed dark brown sugar
- 1 teaspoon kosher salt
- 1 tablespoon ground cinnamon
- 1 teaspoon fresh nutmeg
- 1 teaspoon ginger powder
- ½ teaspoon ground cloves
- ½ teaspoon ground allspice
- 1 teaspoon ancho chile powder (optional)
- 1 (7-ounce) can coconut milk
- 2 tablespoons cornstarch

Preheat the oven to 375°F.

Drain the apples, reserving the liquid and return them to the bowl. In a small saucepan, reduce the liquid over medium heat by half. Remove the pan from the heat and stir in the coconut milk. Set aside.

Toss the apples with the cornstarch, then pour them in a greased 8 x 8-inch casserole dish. Pour the coconut syrup over the apples. Top with enough crumb topping so that the apples are no longer visible. Bake in the preheated oven for 30 minutes.

Turn the pan and bake an additional 20 minutes, or until topping is golden brown and apples are tender. Serve warm with ice cream, whipped cream, or naked.

PEANUT BUTTER PRETZEL BARS

What started out as a Rice Krispie treat got a little offtrack when we decided to add the flavors of a Reese's Peanut Butter Cup. Then, somehow, pretzels got involved. If you want to get really crazy, add a sprinkle of Hawaiian sea salt to the top. The result is rather decadent—a rich, crispy, sweet, salty, and chocolaty delicious mess. Serve these bars chilled, or they'll be even messier.

To make the pretzel crust, lightly spray an 8 x 8-inch casserole dish with pan spray. Cut a piece of parchment into a 6 x 8-inch rectangle. Lay parchment across the width of the casserole dish, allowing the excess to hang over the sides. Set aside.

Place the pretzel pieces in a large, heat-resistant mixing bowl. Add the sugar and corn syrup to a heavy-bottomed 2-quart saucepan. Carefully pour the water into the saucepan, taking care not to splash sugar onto the sides of the pan. Over medium heat, gently stir the mixture to dissolve the sugar. Once the sugar has completely dissolved, stop stirring. Raise heat to medium high and, using a candy thermometer to test the progression of the temperature, let the mixture boil until it reaches 234°F.

Once it has reached temperature, remove the mixture from the heat and carefully stir in the melted butter. Next, pour the syrup with the incorporated butter over the pretzel pieces. Lightly stir with a heat-resistant spatula until all of the pretzel pieces are coated with the syrup.

Dump the mixture into a prepared pan. Cover with parchment paper, and press the mixture until it spreads out into an even layer. Remove the parchment and chill the mixture in a refrigerator for at least 15 minutes.

Yield: 12 bars

For the pretzel crust:

4 cups hard pretzels, rough crushed by hand

¾ cup sugar

½ cup light corn syrup

¼ cup water

4 ounces butter, melted

For the peanut butter ganache:

10 ounces milk chocolate

2 cups creamy peanut butter

For the chocolate ganache:

6 ounces dark chocolate

1 teaspoon light corn syrup

4 ounces butter, cubed

Meanwhile, melt the peanut butter ganache ingredients over a double boiler or in a microwave-safe bowl. Stir to combine. Pour the ganache over the pretzel crust, and then tilt the pan back and forth until the ganache forms an even layer over the crust. Chill for 30 minutes.

Next, melt the chocolate ganache, just like you did the peanut butter ganache. Carefully pour an even layer of chocolate ganache over the peanut butter layer.

Once the chocolate ganache has set, cut around the edges with a paring knife. Lift out the completed product by grasping the excess parchment paper. Place the whole thing onto a cutting board and then cut into 12 or more bars.

Individually wrap and chill for up to a week.

PEANUT BUTTER–BANANA
UPSIDE DOWN CAKE

Yield: 8–10 slices

1¼ cups sugar, divided

1½ cups all-purpose flour

1½ teaspoons
   baking powder

½ teaspoon kosher salt

4 ounces cold, cubed
   butter, plus 4 ounces
   softened butter

2 large eggs

½ teaspoon vanilla extract

½ cup milk

1 cup creamy peanut butter

1 cup dark brown sugar

5 medium-ripe bananas,
   halved lengthwise

On special occasions at home, Chef Shane likes to make peanut butter–banana pancakes. He wanted to bring the same flavor to 12 Bones, but pancakes were already blacklisted (see page 170). So this is our take on a pancake, in cake form. You'll find this cake is light, fluffy, and airy, like a really thick pancake. It's also really moist from the syrup that runs over it when you flip it.

Preheat the oven to 350°F. Grease a 10-inch cake pan and then put ¼ cup of sugar in the pan, rotating it so that the sugar coats the entire inside. Shake out the excess.

In a bowl, whisk together the flour, the baking powder, and the salt. In a stand-up mixer fitted with a paddle attachment, beat 8 ounces of cold butter with the remaining 1 cup of sugar until light and fluffy, about 5 minutes. Beat in the eggs, one at a time, and then the vanilla. In three alternating batches, beat in the flour mixture and the milk. Remove the bowl from the mixer and then stir in the peanut butter with a wooden spoon or a rubber spatula.

In a separate bowl, blend the softened butter with the brown sugar and spread into the bottom of the greased pan. Lay the bananas, cut side up, in a single layer on top of the brown sugar and butter smear. Pour the batter over the bananas. Set the cake pan on a large cookie sheet to catch any spillage.

Bake the cake on the center rack of the oven for approximately 1 hour, or until a toothpick inserted into the middle of the cake comes out clean. Remove the cake from the oven and cool it on a wire rack for about 20 minutes. Place a serving platter or cutting board on top of the cake pan and invert. Carefully pull away the pan, and scrape out any remaining syrup. Slice and serve.

APPLE BRANDY
BUCKLE

This is a mixture of two different recipes, an apple coffee cake and an apple upside down cake. It came about when Bryan's grandfather dropped off a load of rare heirloom apples by the name of Limbertwig. They're small and rough but delicious. They have a perfect sweet-tart taste that's different from most other apples. Just as important in this recipe: Their hard texture holds up well to a long cooking time. If you can't find the somewhat obscure Limbertwig, you can substitute the apples of your choice. A mix of firm but ripe Fujis and Granny Smith apples would do the trick. Whatever you use, it needs to be a hard apple, so stay away from Golden Delicious and Red Delicious varieties.

Preheat the oven to 350°F. Butter and flour a 10-inch springform pan. In a medium size bowl, soak the apples in the brandy. Set aside.

For the topping, in a food processor, pulse the flour, brown sugar, cinnamon, and salt. Add the butter and then process until the mixture resembles moist sand. Add the pecans and pulse three times. Transfer this topping to a baking sheet and then spread and press it down to about a quarter of an inch. A larger surface area will help the topping dry out more thoroughly, and then you can break it into the size you most prefer for the top of the buckle. Leave the topping uncovered in the refrigerator to dry while you make the rest of the cake.

For the buckle, whisk together the flour, baking powder, ground ginger, and salt. In a large bowl, use an electric mixer to beat the butter until it's creamy. Add the sugar and continue to beat until light and fluffy, then beat in the honey and vanilla until everything is well combined. Beat in the eggs, one at a time, then the heavy cream. Fold in the flour mixture with a rubber spatula, and then fold in the apples.

Scrape the batter into the prepared pan. Sprinkle the top of the batter with the topping, and then bake the buckle on the center rack of the oven for 1 hour, or until a toothpick inserted into the middle of the cake comes out clean. Let the cake rest at room temperature for 1 hour before removing the springform ring. Buckle is best at room temperature or warm but can be kept chilled for up to three days.

Serves 8–10

For the crumb topping:

1½ cups all-purpose flour

¾ cup dark brown sugar

1 teaspoon ground cinnamon

4 ounces butter, softened

½ cup pecan pieces

For the buckle:

2 pounds Granny Smith or other hard apples, peeled, cored, and medium diced

1 cup brandy

2 cups all-purpose flour, sifted

2 teaspoons baking powder

¼ teaspoon ground ginger

¼ teaspoon kosher salt

6 ounces butter, softened

½ cup sugar

¼ cup honey

1 teaspoon vanilla extract

2 eggs

½ cup heavy cream

¼ cup candied ginger (page 201), minced

TRES LECHES STRAWBERRY SHORTCAKE

Yield: 10–12 servings

For the cake:

1½ cups all-purpose flour

2 teaspoons baking powder

½ teaspoon salt

3 eggs, room temperature

1 cup sugar

1 teaspoon vanilla extract

½ cup milk, room temperature

For the tres leches:

1½ cup heavy cream

1 12-ounce can of evaporated milk

1 vanilla bean pod, seeds removed

1 cinnamon stick

4 whole cloves

4 whole allspice

1 14-ounce can of sweetened condensed milk

½ teaspoon ground cinnamon

Vanilla seeds from pod

For the topping:

2 pints strawberries

1 cup sugar, divided

4 cups mascarpone cheese

In any restaurant, you'll find yourself working next to many other cultures, and 12 Bones is no exception. This recipe came about after one of our longtime employees from Guadalajara, Yola, brought in the tres leches birthday cake her niece had made for her. The flavors inspired Chef Shane to make this cake, which he says is a cross between strawberry cheesecake, Italian tiramisu, and Mexican tres leches.

This recipe calls for preparing everything in a baking dish and then slicing and serving. At 12 Bones, Chef Shane sometimes uses a piece of PVC pipe as a ring mold, stacking multiple layers inside before removing the pipe. It makes for a lovely presentation if you have the time and inclination (see the photo at left). If not, don't worry about it: This delicious recipe tastes the same either way!

Preheat oven to 350°F. Lightly grease a 9 x 13-inch casserole dish.

In a medium mixing bowl, whisk together the flour, baking powder, and salt. Set aside.

Then in the bowl of a stand-up mixer fitted with a paddle attachment, beat the eggs, sugar, and vanilla extract until light and fluffy—about 5 minutes. Mix in half of the flour mixture on low for 30 seconds, then the milk and remaining flour mixture. Remove the bowl from the mixer, and scrape the bottom and the sides of the bowl with a rubber spatula. Pour the batter into the prepared baking dish, and bake the cake on the center rack of the oven for 20 minutes, or until a toothpick inserted into the middle of the cake comes out clean. Remove the cake from the oven and cool at room temperature on a wire rack for 30 minutes to an hour.

(continued on page 214)

While the cake is cooling, make the tres leches. In a medium saucepan, stir together the cream, evaporated milk, vanilla pod, cinnamon stick, cloves, and allspice. Bring mixture just to a boil, then reduce the heat to low and simmer for 10 minutes. Remove the cream mixture from the heat, then steep it at room temperature, uncovered, for about 30 minutes. In a medium mixing bowl, whisk together the condensed milk, ground cinnamon and vanilla seeds. Using a fine sieve, strain the evaporated milk mixture into the condensed milk mixture. Stir to combine and then poor the liquid over the cake. Cover and chill for at least 4 hours, preferably overnight.

To make the topping, cut out the cores of the strawberries, then quarter them. Toss the berries with ½ cup sugar, then cover and chill them for at least 4 hours. Using a stand-up mixer with the whisk attachment or a handheld mixer, whip the mascarpone cheese and the other ½ cup sugar until the cheese is light and fluffy. Transfer the cheese to a large pastry bag, fitted with a star top. Tie off the end of the bag with a rubber band, and chill until ready to use. Remove the cake and strawberries from fridge. Stir the berries and pour over the cake, along with the rendered juices. Slice the cake into desired-size pieces and doll it up with the mascarpone cheese.

PIE DOUGH

In a stand-up mixer fitted with paddle attachment, mix together flour, sugar, and butter chunks until butter has broken down into pecan-size pieces. In a separate bowl, whisk together yolks and milk, and dump this into the flour mixture. Mix on low for 30 seconds. Lightly flour your work surface. Dump dough onto the work surface, and form it into tight mound. Mash down the mound with the palm of your hand to smear in the butter. Continue until there are no more clumps of butter. Do not over smear. You want streaks of butter in dough. Using a knife or bench scrapper, cut the dough into four pieces. Flatten each dough ball into a disk. Wrap the disks in plastic wrap and chill for at least 2 hours before using. Dough can be frozen for later usage.

3	cups all-purpose flour
2	tablespoons sugar
1	pound butter, cut in approximately 24 pieces and cold
4	egg yolks
⅓	cup milk, cold

ingredient spotlight:
RHUBARB

Though known as a spring vegetable that gets good use in Southern sweets, rhubarb has Asian roots. It was used as a medicinal plant in China, as far back as 2700 B.C. According to the *Rhubarb Compendium*, a group dedicated to tracking the history and uses of the leafy green plant with the distinctive pink stem, rhubarb didn't make its way to the States until the late 18th century. Somewhere between the time that the United States Constitution came into effect and the Louisiana Purchase, a Maine gardener was planting the first rhubarb seeds behind his house. By 1822, rhubarb was sold in produce markets.

Rhubarb has stridently tart stalks, which works hand-in-hand with sweet fruits, such as strawberries, in jams, pies, and other sweets. But its uses aren't limited to dessert, and its tart flavor lends itself well to savory dishes when cooked into sauces and chutneys.

RHUBARB PRESERVES

Yield: About 2 cups

- ¾ cup water
- ¼ cup dark brown sugar
- 1 teaspoon ginger, peeled and grated
- ¼ teaspoon ground allspice
- 1 cinnamon stick
- ½ teaspoon kosher salt
- 1 pound rhubarb stalks, cut into 1-inch pieces

Though we use this recipe for our turnovers, you can use it for anything, including eating it right out of the jar. Most people aren't used to finding rhubarb without its constant companion, strawberries. However, rhubarb also goes great with ginger and cinnamon. This jam has just enough sugar to tone down the tartness of the vegetable, but it still has plenty of tang. If you're looking for rhubarb in the grocery store or farmers' market, make sure that it's firm and not rubbery. Don't refrigerate it while it's still in stalk form and, whatever you do, don't eat the leaves.

In a medium saucepan, stir together all the ingredients, except for the rhubarb. Cook this mixture over medium heat, while stirring constantly, until sugar has dissolved. Stir in the rhubarb pieces, and continue to cook, stirring occasionally, until the mixture thickens into the consistency of jam. This should take about 20 minutes.

Remove the jam from the heat, and let it cool to room temperature. The preserves can be held, covered in the refrigerator, for up to a week.

RHUBARB AND STRAWBERRY
TURNOVERS

Once we were serving two traditional pies by the slice, we started thinking about a way to make pie that's handier to serve in a restaurant when it gets crazy busy—a pie that could make for that perfect grab-and-go dessert. There's a reason that toaster pastries have become the unofficial sugary mascot of rushed breakfasts everywhere. They are made for people on the move. So we decided to create our own take on the toaster pastry, with a filling inspired by strawberry-rhubarb pie, that classic, sweet-tart Southern dessert.

Preheat the oven to 375°F. Line two baking pans with silicone mats or parchment paper, and set aside. Whisk together the egg and water with a fork until well incorporated, then cover and chill. Place one dough disk onto a generously floured work surface. Dust the top of the dough with flour, and roll it into a ¼-inch circle with a rolling pin. This doesn't, of course, have to be a perfect circle. Dust your imperfect circle with a touch of flour, and flip it over. Continue to roll the dough until it is very thin. You should be able to see your work surface through the dough. If the dough begins to stick, dust the top with flour and carefully lift the edges, then flip it onto a freshly floured work surface.

Cut the dough with a 4-inch biscuit cutter by pressing the cutter down through the dough to the work surface and gently twisting. Cut as many disks as you can out of your dough and pull away the scrap—save it if you think you can use it for something else. Carefully transfer the dough to the parchment-lined baking pan. Dust off the excess flour with a pastry brush and refrigerate the disks, uncovered. Repeat this process with the second disk of pie dough.

Yield: About 12 turnovers

- 1 recipe pie dough, cold (page 215)
- All-purpose flour for dusting
- 1 egg
- 1 teaspoon water
- 1 recipe Rhubarb Preserves (page 217)
- 1 cup confectioners sugar
- 1 cup freeze-dried strawberries

While the second pan of dough disks is chilling, remove the first pan from the fridge. Lightly brush the outside edges of the disks with egg wash. Place 1 tablespoon of Rhubarb Preserve in the center of each disk, and spread the preserves around with the back of a spoon, leaving ¼ inch from the edge. Fold the pies in half and crimp the edges with a fork. Place the pies in the fridge and repeat the process with the other pan of dough disks. Once the second completed pan has chilled for 10 minutes, remove both of the pans from the fridge and put all the pies onto one pan. Lightly brush the tops of the pies with the remaining egg wash. Bake in the center of the oven until golden brown, about 20 minutes.

While the pies are baking, put the confectioners sugar in a small bowl, drizzle in a few drops of cold water, and whisk the wet sugar with a fork. Add more water, if necessary, to make a thick, but spreadable, icing. Set aside. Open freeze-dried strawberries, squeeze out the air, and then reseal the bag. Roll over the bag with a rolling pin until the berries are crushed to the consistency of pretzel salt.

Once the pies are done, remove them from the oven and cool them on a wire rack at room temperature for 5 minutes. Then brush the pies with the icing, then generously sprinkle with the crushed strawberries. Allow the icing to set before serving. The pies are best served warm or at room temperature. Leftovers can be stored in an airtight container in the fridge for up to two days, then brought back to room temperature before serving.

CHOCOLATE WHISKEY CAKE
WITH COFFEE BEAN GANACHE

Chocolate and whiskey go hand-in-hand. That's why Chef Shane has tried to replace some of the liquid mix of a variety of chocolate desserts with whiskey just to see how they'd turn out. When he tried this chocolate cake for the first time, he knew he had a hit on his hands.

The bittersweet ganache adds balance to the sweet cake. The coffee also adds an extra element of aroma and depth to the flavor. Also, ganache creates a sort of tasty shell for the interior, which helps keeps the cake moist.

Preheat the oven to 350°F. Lightly spray a 10-inch springform pan with nonstick spray. Wrap the outside of the pan tightly with aluminum foil to prevent leakage. Mix together in a medium saucepan the sugar, chocolate, butter, and whiskey. Stir over low heat until the butter and the chocolate have melted. Remove from heat and let cool slightly.

For the cake:
In a medium bowl sift together flour, baking soda, baking powder, and salt. In a large bowl, stir together the milk and vinegar. Whisk the vanilla and the eggs into the milk mixture, then whisk in the chocolate-whiskey mixture. Fold in the dry ingredients a little bit at a time with a rubber spatula, then pour the batter, once mixed, into the prepared pan. Bake in the center of the oven until a skewer inserted in the middle of the cake comes out clean, about 40 minutes. Remove the cake from the oven and let it cool on a wire rack before unhinging the springform pan.

For the ganache:
While the cake is cooling, make the ganache. Combine all the ingredients except for the coffee in a double boiler with the water barely simmering. Once everything is melted, remove from heat and stir in the ground coffee.

Once the cake is released from the pan, place it on a serving platter. Then, pour the ganache over the cake, letting the sauce run over the sides. Allow the sauce to cool and set at room temperature—about 30 minutes. To slice, dip a knife in hot water, then wipe the water off with a clean, dry towel before cutting the cake. Repeat this for every slice.

The cake can be covered and kept in the fridge for up to five days, or kept at room temperature for two days.

Yield: About 10 slices

For the cake:

2 cups sugar

4 ounces unsweetened chocolate

4 ounces butter

1 cup whiskey

2 cups all-purpose flour

2 teaspoons baking soda

1 teaspoon baking powder

1 teaspoon kosher salt

1 cup whole milk

1 teaspoon cider vinegar

1 teaspoon vanilla extract

2 eggs

For the ganache:

6 ounces bittersweet chocolate, fine-chopped

1 teaspoon corn syrup

4 ounces butter, softened

1 tablespoon coarse-ground coffee beans

INDEX

ABOUT THE AUTHORS

BRYAN AND ANGELA KING are the co-owners of 12 Bones Smokehouse, where **SHANE HEAVNER** is the head chef. Over the past decade, 12 Bones has quickly grown into an Asheville institution known best for its rule-breaking take on barbecue classics, such as their Blueberry Chipotle Baby Back Ribs. The restaurant has been featured in a variety of national media, from magazines like *Southern Living* and *Garden & Gun* to television networks like ABC, NBC, and the Travel Channel.

MACKENSY LUNSFORD is a food writer, journalist, and a former chef and restaurant owner. She has covered Southern restaurants for a variety of independently owned media and more recently for Gannett newspapers. She has won numerous journalism awards from The North Carolina Press Association and is a first place national award winner for food writing from the Association of Alternative Newsweeklies. Lunsford also writes and develops recipes for The Coca-Cola Company.

ACKNOWLEDGMENTS
FROM BRYAN KING, ANGELA KING, AND SHANE HEAVNER

We would like to thank the following people. Without them, 12 Bones would not exist:

Tom and Sabra, for their vision in creating 12 Bones as well as
for their invaluable guidance, insight, and advice.

Joe Lewis, our south store head chef, for his inspiration, creativity,
and willingness to constantly go above and beyond.

Our family of employees, past and present, who have contributed immeasurably
to 12 Bones' success and growth with their hard work, dedication, and passion.
12 Bones is truly a special place because of your efforts.

Our loyal patrons, from near and far, who have supported 12 Bones
since it was just a little barbecue joint down by the river.

Our friends and families, notably Bryan's parents, Lee and Sarah, and Shane's wife, Jess.
You all have always been there for us through thick and thin as we continue to learn and give
tremendously of ourselves in the hope that 12 Bones will prosper forever—but never forget its
down-home roots. We love you all and look forward to what the future holds with your support.
Mackensy Lunsford, for putting up with us enough to compile all of our recipes, thoughts, and
stories into this cookbook in a manner that people will want to read. You brought energy and
enthusiasm to the project and we are incredibly proud of the result. To say we couldn't have done
it without you would be an understatement.

ACKNOWLEDGMENTS
FROM MACKENSY LUNSFORD

This book is dedicated to Clarence Lunsford: family man, gardener,
occasional grouch, and all-around wonderful person.

Thanks go to my friends and family members who remain patient even as I disappear for months
at a time to work on projects such as these. To my husband, Eric Steineger, the kindest and most
patient man I've ever met. The house surely would have fallen apart without you (and I might have,
too). To my grandmother, Maryanne Lunsford, and my parents, who have always believed in me,
even when the road I traveled was far from conventional. And to the crew at 12 Bones, who put up
with my bossiness throughout the creation of this book.